Those Who Can't...
A Teacher's Gap Years

In and Out of post-Communist Poland

Published by Green Publications

Copyright © 2018 Adam Tangent

Adam Tangent has asserted his right
under the Copyright, Designs and Patents Act 1988
to be identified as the author of this work.

ISBN 978-1-98619-880-6

Also available as a Kindle ebook
ISBN 978-1-84396-504-6

A catalogue record for
this book is available from the British Library
and the American Library of Congress

Cover design and artwork
Paul Morris
www.mostlygreenstuff.com

Pre-press production
eBook Versions
27 Old Gloucester Street
London WC1N 3AX

For Waldek and AWP

Those Who Can't...
A Teacher's Gap Years

In and Out of post-Communist Poland

Adam Tangent

GREEN PUBLICATIONS

Chapter One
Leicester – Toruń / Waldek / Shopping /
Mercy Schwimmer / The Ruffs

In March 1990 I finally received two offers of permanent employment. Blockbuster Video were opening a big new store on London Road and the manager, Mike, was quick to offer me a job.

'I need you here early Saturday morning. There's going to be builders and all sorts of shite crawling round here. I want you to hold the fort till I get here. Good lad.'

Mike didn't pretend to be interested in my post-graduate research and conducted the informal interview on his terms. 'If Robson (the Managing Director) says he wants those boxes shifted I'll do it myself. I don't mind getting covered in crap if I am taking home thirty k. You did a degree – fair play to you – but what are you earning now?'

There was no post-graduate research but I needed a cover story to explain my sudden conversion to 'retail' and 'the product' (videos). I also felt it necessary to show Mike that I was in it for the long haul, and so described my 'research' as 'a slow boat to China', as if he cared.

In fact I managed only six weeks. This was more than

Assistant Managers Rob and Graham, sacked after only a few weeks in a ruthless cull, and more than I had expected after a rowdy Saturday night visit from some friends loudly asking for 'that film Bumfuckers'. I promised Mike it would never happen again and was given a second chance.

There was also an offer from a Professor Pawlik to teach in the Department of English Philology at Nicolaus Copernicus University in Toruń, Poland. I met his envoy, Mr Krzeszewski, on the fourteenth floor of the Humanities building at the University. A thin man wearing a bobble hat and large glasses stepped out of the paternoster.

There was something rather goofy about him, which – despite his heavy accent and serious manner – quickly put me at my ease. It also helped that none of the other post-graduate students (post post-graduate in my case) to whom the job had been advertised had applied. Mr Krzeszewski kept his bobble hat on throughout our meeting. Basically the job was mine if I wanted it.

Neither appointment impressed my two housemates. Alan, contemplating a move to London and an investment in sun bed rental, was particularly critical. 'Poland! Fucking hell mate. What do you want to go to Poland for? You're better off sticking at Blockbusters.' Alistair joined in but at least promised to visit.

Mr Krzeszewski was there to meet me at the railway station when I arrived in Toruń towards the end of September. We squeezed ourselves uncomfortably into his tiny Fiat, whilst my luggage followed on behind in a taxi, and drove to the flat provided for me by the university.

At no stage had it been a comfortable journey. In Dover I

had been cheerfully informed of a rail strike disrupting trains out of Ostend. This was to be miraculously lifted minutes before the departure of my train to Warsaw, but the prospect of an unscheduled stay in Belgium had done nothing to brighten the three-hour crossing. I settled down in my compartment in the company of an Austrian Mormon and an Irishman who kept repeating 'Yes' to himself every few seconds. He was on his way to see the Berlin wall before it was pulled down but constantly fretted about being on the wrong train. In the end he and the Austrian got off the train somewhere in Belgium. Otherwise there seemed to be virtually nobody on the train until we stopped in Berlin early the following morning, when the compartment – which I had come to regard as my own – filled with suspicious looking strangers.

At the Polish border soldiers boarded the train demanding passports and visas. I had no visa only a typed letter from the university. The first soldier muttered something about a 'problem' and disappeared with my passport. Other soldiers passed through the train double-checking everyone's papers but this time I couldn't even produce my passport. I expected at any moment to be led off of the train in disgrace. Eventually the soldiers returned with a hurriedly issued visa and a bill for 442,000 złoty! They agreed to take sterling and I prepared to part with all of my hard currency. In fact, the train was held in the station whilst the soldier went off to check the exchange rate, returning a few minutes later with a bill for £26. Was this an act of clemency, I wondered. Perhaps it was merely a down payment and the visa proper would have to be applied for later on arrival. I was delighted, therefore, when the soldier re-appeared with my change – 68,000 złoty (or £4).

The train finally got going again and I returned to my compartment to cold stares all round. Outside the landscape seemed to become more and more dismal: flat scrubby plains – perfect for a tank battle – interspersed with heavy tracts of forest; there were no friendly hedgerows, just vast unkempt grassland. All I had seen of Poland previously were the dark snow covered streets behind the BBC correspondent Tim Sebastian, from his reports during martial law, and also footage of the Gdańsk shipyard during the *Solidarity* strike – pictures of men with checked shirts and moustaches sleeping inside the shipyard buildings. I had been expecting heavy industry and blocks of grim apartments not open country with an occasional farmer toiling behind a horse and plough.

Towards midday we stopped in a desolate looking siding. Passengers got out and smoked and local men moved through the compartments selling bottles of beer from old sports bags. Had I known it, my change for the visa could have bought the entire contents of one well-stocked bag.

A couple of hours later, in Poznań, I boarded an even slower train which took me the rest of the way to Toruń.

'So we will go now, erm, to your neighbour Waldek Skrzypek,' Mr Krzeszewski said as we arrived at my flat. He might have added 'who lives next door', but instead left me to contemplate folding myself back into his Fiat.

By the time I arrived in Toruń, Professor Pawlik had left for America and a visiting professorship. He had, it appeared, still found time to arrange my reception; I was to put myself entirely in the hands of Waldek, to whose apartment and warm welcome I was delivered that first evening.

'Ahhhh. Mr Adam! Let me look at you. Please come in. Yes, please sit here.'

Waldek ushered me to the leather chair in which he placed all visitors and then disappeared, returning shortly after with a tray of snacks and a bottle of vodka.

After a few pleasantries – I was invited for tea the following day – Mr Krzeszewski made his excuses and left. Waldek, with his black linen suit and cigarettes seemed terribly cosmopolitan by comparison and was, I imagined, an *East European intellectual,* albeit one playing *Chris Rea's Greatest Hits.*

Waldek shared his small flat with his wife Basia and their precociously musical daughter Emilia, but had made the living room his own. Instead of the usual 70s' wall unit, Waldek housed his books on *cognitive linguistics* in an elegant teak bureau. An almost antique typewriter sat on the leather-covered desktop and there was a piano and a classical guitar.

This didn't seem to be the time to ask what was really on my mind. *'But what am I to teach them?'* asks the timid hero of Evelyn Waugh's novel *Decline and Fall.* My teaching experience up to this point consisted of two weeks teaching English to a small group of Austrian boys who were attending a residential school during the Easter holidays. During the dark days at Blockbuster Video I had dutifully applied to do a PGCE (Post Graduate Certificate of Education). My first choice had been Leicester University's School of Education, but after an extremely short interview I had received a letter of rejection. In fact the course tutor terminated my interview after two minutes, after I had admitted, rather unwisely, that I didn't actually want to be a teacher but that I needed 'something lined up for next year'. Instead of dressing smartly I had worn jeans and the customised donkey jacket I wore for all other occasions. For my second interview at Nottingham University I swapped this for a suit and tie and tried to say all the right things. It worked and they even let me put off doing the course for a year so that I could go to Poland.

Waldek, however, had just returned from an academic conference at Keele University, and spoke expansively of his PhD research; he was clearly not the person to whom I should reveal my anxiety. (In fact the answer from Captain Grimes – *'Oh, I shouldn't try to teach them anything, not just yet anyway.'* – was closer to Waldek's relaxed work ethic than I could have appreciated.)

For now though, I was reluctant to part with my man-of-the-world status – implicit I liked to think in the bottle of vodka – and so drank my share as if pickled cucumbers and bison grass vodka were all standard procedure.

The next morning I was woken by the rattle of the trams passing in the street below. Soon after Waldek arrived to take me to the university. First to the rectorate building on the main campus where I was to be processed as a university employee and then to the Collegium Maius in the old town where I would be teaching. Among the introductions was an encounter with the keeper of the photocopier – situated in a kind of prison cell deep in the basement. He seemed rather put out that I wasn't German but continued to speak German to me anyway. He persisted on my subsequent visits and I invariably came away with the wrong pages and the sound of him tutting loudly in his chair.

The Collegium Maius was a huge dark building on four

floors. The English Department was situated on the third floor and by the time we reached it Waldek was breathing heavily and perspiring in his thick leather coat. The start of term was still more than two weeks away and the building was almost completely empty and yet Professor Pawlik had insisted on my early arrival. Having thrown over my oldest friend's wedding to be there on time I was somewhat dismayed to discover that not only was the Professor missing but that the rest of the department were still enjoying their holidays. The other British native speaker joining the department would also not be arriving for another week, Waldek informed me over a pizza in the Old Town – a Mr Ruff and his wife. This evoked a succession of homely images – being invited to have my tea with the older couple, kindly Mrs Ruff bringing out an apple crumble for pudding – and I immediately suggested that I should accompany Waldek when he went to meet them the following week.

Until then, however, I continued to monopolise Waldek's sitting room. When I visited him that evening he was in high spirits. Basia was out at work and there was a gleam in his eye as he re-appeared carrying a bottle of vodka on a silver tray. It was still light outside and a warm breeze blew in through the open door to the balcony. Waldek put on a Chris Rea tape and sat back with a sigh of contentment.

'Ah Adam! While the cat's away... cheers! Let me bring you something to eat. Some cheese? Some sausage perhaps?'

When he returned from the kitchen Waldek attempted to explain his PhD thesis. It would have to be completed within the next couple of years or there might be problems remaining in the flat – technically in the gift of the university. Through the haze of vodka I pretended to follow what he was saying. What was *cognition*, I wondered?

As the evening wore on Waldek grew more sentimental. 'You know, Adam, you will find things in Poland very different to what you are used to. Everything here must seem very grey to you. All of the buildings are dirty and peeling, but for me it's beautiful. Poland is a poor country but it has wonderful forests and lakes. On Saturday you must come with us to the forest to pick mushrooms.'

This was a more significant invitation than I at first appreciated. Before going to Poland someone had told me, rather dismissively, that beetroot was the national dish. Mushrooms, in all their infinite varieties, were in fact the real source of pride amongst Poles and superior laughter greeted anyone who dared to ask the Polish word for mushrooms. 'You mean *pieczarki*. But we have so many other varieties of mushroom here in Poland.' Real mushrooms, it seemed, only grew wild in the forest.

Even urban Poles, who otherwise showed no affinity with the countryside, claimed intimate knowledge of the fungi growing in Polish forests. Being able to tell which were edible and which were not seemed to be a matter of national pride – a proof of their Polishness. There is even a mushroom picking scene in Poland's national epic poem *Pan Tadeusz* (or to give it its full title in English, *Sir Thaddeus or the Last Lithuanian Forray: A Nobleman's Tale from the Years of 1811 and 1812 in Twelve Books of Verse*). This appears in *Book Three: Flirtations*, in which there is clearly more to mushrooms than just fungus:

Mushrooms abounded – round the fair damsels the young men did throng;
Or vixens, as they're hailed in Lithuanian song.
They symbolise maidenhood, their flesh no maggot bites...

At the weekend, as he had promised, we drove out to a dark pine forest. It was damp and pleasantly spongy underfoot and whilst Basia and Emilia collected mushrooms Waldek and I stood around chatting.

'Professor Pawlik is a very clever man, Adam. He has his own way of making sure things are done. He can be very formal but really I like him. Waldemar, he will say, can I leave you to make the arrangements for the native speakers. He has a lot of influence with the Rector of the University so I am always happy to help him.'

Although I was soon to become a fan of all things Polish, I was initially deeply suspicious of everything. I avoided all dairy products and only shopped at *Edward Śmigielski's*, a mini western-style supermarket about the size of an average SPAR shop, where I paid hugely inflated prices for imported food products from West Germany. My first purchase was a large and very expensive tin of dried milk, a necessary alternative to the local bottled milk with its head of curdled cream. A more refined product was sold in infuriatingly floppy plastic bags, most of which ended up on the floor or in the fridge.

I didn't attempt to make a phone call or use my washing machine and shunned the tramline which ran outside my apartment block. I had located the British Council Library, however, and spent much of the first fortnight reading British campus novels in between snacks of packet soups and cheese sandwiches.

I soon realised I would not be able to shop exclusively at *Smigielski's*. The advantage of shopping there, as in Tesco or Sainsbury's, was that one wasn't required to speak. Customers were trusted to pick items from the shelves themselves and enjoyed the freedom of walking around with them in a basket before paying. The alternative to exorbitant prices and decadent western practices was the traditional *sklep*. In the communist spirit of queuing/jobs for the girls, a *sklep* involved visiting/ queuing at three or four different counters and communicating with three or four different depressed shop assistants. The anonymous packaging – thick brown paper for most items not in a tin or the fridge – didn't help either, making it impossible for the silent shopper to distinguish sugar from flour, lentils from eggs etc.

An alternative to packet soup and sandwiches were the university *stołówkas*. These were the several canteens which catered for anyone connected or who had ever been connected with the university. Waldek had seen to it that I was given a book of tickets. This entitled me to a three course lunch in what, until the students returned, resembled a pensioners' club. There was generally pale, unpalatable soup and a main course of fried meat accompanied by cabbage and grated carrot. In case anyone should think of stealing the cutlery the point of each knife had been removed.

It was on my way to the *stołówka*, invariably under leaden grey skies, that I first entertained thoughts of Mercy Schwimmer – an American girl whom Waldek had mentioned on my first evening in Toruń. He was clearly quite taken with her and I imagined an uncomplicated American girl, hungry for contact with the west. She would need the company as much as I did, I reasoned. Waldek had mentioned to her that we were neighbours and she was keen to meet me.

One evening, a week or so after my arrival, I presented myself at her door to press my claim. The door was opened by a young man with blonde hair.

'Who is it?' called a voice from inside. I wasn't prepared for this, nor for Mercy Schwimmer to appear at the man's shoulder in matching sweatshirt and pants in a pose of unmistakable intimacy. I could hardly back out now and so blundered on, accepting their rather startled invitation to a cup of tea.

'Do we have tea, Piotrek?'

Whilst Piotrek – the boyfriend – made the tea she curled up unattractively on the settee. I explained my connection with Waldek.

'Is that the guy from Collegium Maius? He taught the first week of Peace Corps. Are you here with a programme?'

'No. I got the job through my university.'

'Cool.'

In fact she could hardly have looked and sounded less interested. She and Piotrek had met through Peace Corps – a do-gooding arm of American imperialism designed, it seemed, to make white middle class college kids feel like missionaries. Piotrek was a local undergraduate student who'd been engaged to teach them Polish, and was, even now I suspected, planning his passage to the United States. I could not account for their affair in any other way. Mercy Schwimmer was nothing like the girl of my imaginings and after twenty minutes of scratching around for conversation (during which I somehow also managed to break her table lamp) I trudged back to my flat, cursing Waldek as I went.

Until term started in October, he remained, however, my only contact with the outside world. Hardly anyone, it appeared, spoke English and conversation was confined to Waldek, Mr Krzeszewski and a melancholy engineer I met one day at lunch in the *stołówka*. Leaning secretively across the table he whispered, 'We have lots of pretty girls in Poland', before retreating to his soup with a sigh and a look of deep disgust. He continued to watch me out of the corner of his eye but we ate the rest of our lunch in silence. Fortunately, Waldek was an excellent host and whenever Basia was working nights at the nursing college, we would go to a bar in the old town. These were generally deserted but contained hidden dangers according to Waldek.

'Which *dive* are we to visit tonight?' Waldek would ask in his plumy English accent. Inside he would point out 'ladies of the night' and over large tumblers of vodka regaled me with tales of unlikely foreign academics and of his own exploits – busking to a captivated audience in Paris, brushes with the old communist authorities, a night in a police cell, and the emotion he felt on finally being able to travel to England.

The only threatening behaviour in the local bars came from the hawk-eyed women who manned the toilets. The price of a piss in 1990 was 500 złoty – about four pence. Nevertheless I regarded this as an outrageous scam and bitterly resented paying. The 'Sorry, I am a foreigner' line didn't cut any ice and nor did getting haughty with the toilet woman who rattled a tin of coins as you emerged from the cubicle. In the public toilets in the old square a woman sat doing crosswords behind a counter directly opposite the urinals. Having paid, I sometimes found it hard to go if she was watching or if she got up to change the channel on her portable TV.

Towards the end of the evening a mixture of vodka and emotion generally got the better of Waldek and we would stumble home, often shrouded in thick fog. Sometimes Waldek would amble off behind a bush to relieve himself – or 'to check his bicycle' as he put it – and would disappear for what seemed like an age, giggling to himself from behind the bush as he recited his favourite English phrases.

Waldek often re-appeared the next morning with two bottles of beer. As I always refused his hair of the dog cure he would drink both bottles in between a pantomime of groaning and head clutching.

Rather more useful was the map of Toruń Waldek drew for me. With Mercy Schwimmer taken I had the best part of two weeks to explore the city. Inexplicably I had travelled to Poland without a guidebook so for a while Waldek's ornate map was my only reference point. Emblazoned with the city's crest and a medieval looking compass it was a thing of beauty and I was reluctant to risk it on my daily excursions into the old town. The only street names which I recognised or could pronounce were *ul. Gargarina* (after the Soviet astronaut) and of course *ul. Kopernika.* (Guidebook entries for Toruń start with 'the birthplace of Copernicus' and then work their way down, laying claim to Poland's second largest bell and ending with the city's reputation for fine gingerbread.)

The old town was dominated by a long pedestrianised high street which joined the *Rynek Staromiejski* (old town square), with its statue of Copernicus and imposing fourteenth century Town Hall, and the rather less grand *Rynek Nowomiejski* (new square), where it is said Napoleon once stayed overnight. The name and more particularly the width of this street gave rise to 'szeroka dupa' – a popular local insult meaning your bottom is as wide as Szeroka Street. Running parallel to *ul. Szeroka,* two hundred metres away, was the medieval city wall, and beyond that the Vistula river. Because the railway station was on the other side of the river behind a bank of trees, one's first impression was of having arrived in a deserted hamlet. Only when you were crossing the iron bridge over the river did you get a view of the city – the red-brick of the Gothic churches, the Town Hall and the Collegium Maius, and between them the narrow tops of Renaissance houses.

Thankfully, this didn't include Rubinkowo. Depressing even by Polish standards, Toruń's largest and ugliest residential district housed the majority of the city's two hundred thousand inhabitants in enormous blocks of shoebox size apartments. There was never, fortunately, any need to visit Rubinkowo, except to check that what the locals said of it was true. It was indeed hideously ugly but sensibly situated a safe distance from the city centre.

Having cast the Ruffs in solid middle age I was somewhat taken-aback when a young couple holding a baby emerged from the train at Toruń station. 'Daughter' hadn't implied baby.

Understandably tired and a little tetchy, they didn't seem overly pleased to see me either. Unfolding the pram for Natalia was proving difficult and although Waldek made soothing noises it was all rather fraught.

Waldek went with Sarah and Natalia in one taxi and Richard Ruff and I followed behind in another. He seemed extremely cagey. There was certainly no home counties' camaraderie, no mutual pleasure in finding a fellow Brit on foreign soil as one might imagine passing between two Welshman ('Alright Taffy. How you doin boy?') or two Geordies ('Howay Geordie!'). In the land of Solidarność we made tight-lipped small talk until the taxi pulled up at Dom Studencki Ten.

Whilst Waldek showed them around their tiny apartment I hovered in the background feeling smug. The Ruffs had been given a flat roughly half the size of my own and were clearly none too pleased.

Waldek and I left them to it, although he was to return later that evening after being summoned by Richard – unhappy that the two-roomed apartment he'd been promised consisted of one small room divided by a tall shelf unit. For Waldek, who had begun family life in the same block, this touched a raw nerve, and he was brimming with emotion when he visited me the next day.

'I tell you, Adam, that I found the way Richard spoke to me quite offensive. Really, I found it quite unpleasant. I am sure that he is a good man and he is only protecting his family but let me tell you, Basia and I lived very happily in this sort of apartment.'

Waldek couldn't arrange alternative accommodation and nor could he butter-up Richard with effusive hospitality. Rebuffed, he took to mimicking Richard's standard reply to offers of help, 'No, thank you, Waldek. I have my phrasebook.'

The negative opinion I formed of the Ruffs that first evening didn't last long. Richard could certainly come over as a bit of a cold fish – hardly unique for English people – but in fact they were both extremely pleasant. They were both formidably intellectual, and Richard definitely seemed destined for an academic career. It was harder to concentrate on Sarah's theorising because it was usually delivered with Natalia guzzling at her ample bosom. Natalia, or Tashka, showed no inclination for bottled milk and Sarah was happy to oblige, producing a bare breast on demand in the forthright manner of someone throwing down the gauntlet. I quickly learnt not to stray below eye level during conversation or take offence when Sarah wasn't listening because Natalia was saying something more interesting.

Chapter Two

Teaching / Aśka / Warsaw / Conversation

The curtain raiser for the new academic year was a visit from Lech Wałęsa, Poland's President in waiting. Although about to be given the university's Honoury Doctorate, teachers and students were ambivalent about him. Waldek for one couldn't understand how a man with such appalling grammar could receive a distinction of this sort. This was fairly typical of the embarrassment felt by educated Poles towards their national symbol. Despite his misgivings Waldek managed to rustle up three tickets for the ceremony. Basia glammed up for the occasion with a short black skirt and long leather boots but Waldek kept his suit hidden under his raincoat. This was my first opportunity to observe *en masse* the inability of Polish men to look smart, and sat amongst the sea of cheap suits – mainly in brown and grey and worn with incongruous shoes and sweaters – I felt quite dapper in my Chinos and tweed jacket.

After the ceremony Wałęsa's motorcade took him to the old town square. The evening news showed him delivering a fiery oration from an upstairs window in the *ratusz* (town hall).

His aids crowded round him on the small balcony and with the help of a hand held microphone he held court to the locals packed into the square below. It was hard to tell what they made of his performance. There was a lot of finger wagging and the manner of a rather tired man prodding a sleeping man in the way he addressed the crowd.

The following day term began in earnest. Richard and I were introduced to the rest of the Department of English Philology at a meeting overseen by Professor Zielińska, who was to run the department in Professor Pawlik's absence. In her appearance and in her style of management she reminded me of Miss Havisham. Heavily masked by white powder she flicked between high-pitched coquetry and frosty condescension. The latter was mainly reserved for the Polish men in the department – Waldek, Mr Krzeszewski, Zbyszek and the new boy Bartek. Richard and I were spared the worst of this and Richard even enjoyed a measure of respect. Meanwhile the three youngish women lecturers were petted and favoured.

Marek, the librarian, lived in permanent fear of Professor Zielińska and rolled his eyes towards the ceiling whenever I mentioned her name. He was always noticeably more chatty on Wednesdays and Thursdays when he knew she was safely back in Warsaw. Unlike Miss Havisham, Professor Zielińska was not a fixture in her kingdom, in fact appearing for a couple of days only once every fortnight. On her next visit she requested that I meet her from the station to assist in carrying some books. She made a great show of taking a taxi to the Collegium Maius and I felt obliged to put on a show of gratitude for the set of old fashioned textbooks.

I began my teaching that afternoon with a flurry of questions cribbed from a book I'd read on literary theory.

'What is *literature*?'

'OK. What do we do when we study *literature*?'

'This class is called *texts*. What do we mean by *a literary text*?'

'What do we mean by *meaning*? What do we mean by *the meaning of a text*? Perhaps it would help if I spoke more slowly.'

Eventually, one of them asked, 'I am sorry. What is it you want from us?'

But my pedagogy had not yet taken the *student* into account. I was much more concerned with appearing reasonably knowledgeable. For the second *texts* class that afternoon I decided to dispense with the pretence of a dialogue and gave a lecture instead, answering my own questions as I went.

The first thing I noticed about the second class was the addition of male faces. Their manner of entering the room was slightly less mournful than the all-girl group who had just filed out and generally the atmosphere was lighter. One girl, however, appeared to have been crying. She didn't seem to welcome my expressions of concern so I ploughed straight back into 'What is literature?'

After about forty-five minutes one of the students reminded me it was customary to take a half-time break (classes were generally an hour and a half). Towards the end of the break a small committee, led by the girl who had been crying, came up to speak to me. They had been talking amongst themselves and could I start my lesson again as most of the class hadn't understood what I was saying. The girl had stopped crying and was confident and articulate, and worse still extremely attractive.

After the lesson, feeling somewhat deflated, I wandered into the old town behind some of the students. Eager to make conversation I asked them where I could get my hair cut. One of the boys dutifully gave me directions whilst the sad girl who had caught my eye listened impassively.

I had no intention of attempting to communicate with a Polish barber at this stage and so turned for home instead after pretending to head off in the direction shown.

I was to teach *texts, writing* and *conversation* but the question of what exactly I was to teach remained troublingly vague. There was no curriculum and the 'native speakers', as we were known, were left entirely to our own devices.

But at least by Wednesday lunchtime I had finished my teaching for the week. That evening I accompanied Waldek and Basia to a bar on the main campus where Waldek's friend, a local disc jockey/celebrity, was performing with his blues group. The bar was packed with students. Waldek's friend and the band's front man sang the blues in very gruff Polish and played endless harmonica solos, all of which were applauded rapturously.

Going into the concert I had spotted the sad girl from the *texts* class hanging around the entrance to the bar. She turned up again later when the band had finished. I was talking with one of her classmates having ungraciously dumped Waldek for young female company at the first opportunity. The sad girl's name was Joanna, or Aśka. Her classmate had introduced her somewhat reluctantly and there generally seemed little love lost between them. We were also joined later by a shady looking boy whom the girls referred to as *Devil.* He had a pointed beard and a very unpleasant look about him. He was also extremely drunk and on the rare occasions when he spoke (in Polish) provoked outrage from the two girls. When the bar finally closed I gallantly offered to walk them back to their student hostel and with *Devil* in silent pursuit we set off through a small forest. Under a full moon the leaves of the trees glistened with the beginnings of a frost. At one point we had to stop to 'do the swallow', which involved leaning forwards with arms outstretched whilst balancing on one leg. The idea of this was to see whether or not you were sober but with *Devil* not far behind I was relieved when we got going again and emerged from the forest onto the main road. After walking the other girl to her door I accompanied Aśka the rest of the way to *Dom Studencki One.* Before saying goodnight she suggested I might like to see the remains of the Teutonic castle. She would be happy to take me there on Saturday if I wasn't doing anything.

Aśka shared her room in the student hostel with two other girls. Neither were there when I called on Saturday afternoon and I eagerly accepted her offer of a drink. As at Waldek's, this inevitably entailed more than just a drink. Aśka cut some slices of bread and produced a tin of *pasztet* – a rough fatty looking pate, served out of a tin in meaty chunks. Although it looked rather like cat food it actually tasted very good and I tucked in enthusiastically, determined to make a good impression.

Much of our outing on Saturday afternoon passed in silence. During a particularly long pause in the conversation, which lasted the width of the iron road bridge, I started to feel slightly resentful. Having invited me to inspect what amounted to a brick wall she might at least make the effort to speak to me,

I reasoned. Determined to wrestle the initiative I insisted on buying Aśka an ice cream at the smart hotel I had visited with Mr Krzeszewski and his wife the previous weekend. Feeling like the rich foreigner I watched as Aśka ate the Polish equivalent of a Knickerbocker Glory. Now seemed like the right time for a stab at intimacy and so as nonchalantly as I could I asked, 'So, have you got a boyfriend then, Aśka?'

'My boyfriend said he loved me but he has gone to England.'

'Oh right. Is he coming back?' I asked casually.

But this clearly wasn't a conversation Aśka wanted to have. She looked flustered and I felt rather stupid. When Aśka had finished her ice cream we left.

The following Saturday I went to Warsaw with Richard and Sarah. Richard wanted to spend the day in the British Council Library and I was to see the sights with Sarah and Tashka.

The guidebook I'd read before leaving England described a ramshackle railway system and I'd imagined something on the lines of trains in the sub-continent. Departure times, it suggested (quite wrongly), were something of a lottery. Perhaps the Ruffs had read the same book because there was still no sign of them as the train pulled into the station dead on time. Just as I was beginning to despair Richard appeared on the opposite platform, scooting along behind Tashka's pushchair. Sarah, whom he had left buying the tickets, arrived soon after breathing fire. The woman in the ticket office had charged them a child's fare for Tashka and had refused to be intimidated.

Sarah was still bristling when we got to our compartment. This was another in a succession of run-ins she'd had with local Polish women, usually over the vexed question of Tashka's lack of winter clothing. Given how cold winter would get it was perplexing to see local people wrapping up in large coats and hats at the start of October. Local women Sarah met in the park or in shops pointed and tutted disapprovingly if Tashka was showing an inch of bare leg or was not wearing a hat.

During the three hour journey the Ruffs subjected me to a thorough interrogation. Straightforward questions about home, family and why I'd come to Poland took the form of critical scrutiny. As I spoke Richard nodded slowly and said, 'Right. Right,' but sounded deeply sceptical.

'You know that won't really do. The decision making process is always much more complicated than you suggest.'

'Leave him alone Richard. Stop being so nosey.'

The restaurant car provided a welcome change of subject. At the table next to us two businessmen in green suits were eating steak tartare topped by a raw egg. Richard announced that he was going to try it as well.

'I'd rather you didn't Richard. It looks absolutely disgusting.'

'But don't you think as we're here we should try it?'

'Fine. You have it Richard but Tashka and I are having scrambled eggs.'

Outside a succession of nondescript and uniformly grey towns flashed by. Communist town planning housed the workers cheek-by-jowl with their factories. There were no out of town industrial estates, hidden discretely behind poplar trees; instead blocks of flats backed on to railway sidings and overlooked decrepit industrial plant.

Our first stop in Warsaw was a hat shop tucked away in the courtyard of a building opposite the central station. The shop specialised in Lenin hats and Richard wanted one for the winter.

Back out on the street we said goodbye to Richard and headed for the old town. The area near the station was dominated by the huge Palace of Culture, Stalin's gift to the Poles after World War II. A debate was going on in Poland as to its future, one I had tried to get my conversation class to enter into – somebody mentioned knocking it down completely and somebody had heard of a plan to encase it in glass but that was it. Cut into the tower were what looked like gloomy portals, behind which you could easily imagine terrible things being done to the enemies of communism. Thoughts of Room 101 sprang to mind and I found my eyes drawn to the upper rooms.

The long street which led up to the old town was much more cheerful and in pleasant late summer sunshine Sarah warmed to her subject – Richard.

'He can be absolutely dreadful, you know. Last year when he was finishing off his PhD he was appalling. A total shit. It's a miracle we're still together. His family's mad. They're very nice but they're all completely barmy. And they drink like fish.'

Sarah had already spent a year in Poland, teaching at the university in Łódź (pronounced *wooj*). She could speak what seemed to me very proficient Polish and when we stopped in a restaurant for lunch translated the menu for me before continuing her story. Tashka had been conceived when Richard visited her that Christmas. Richard had then returned to York and his PhD leaving Sarah pregnant and the object of some curiosity.

In this confessional atmosphere I told Sarah about my apple crumble fantasy and she promised to cook one with a Sunday roast.

After lunch Sarah and I walked the rest of the way to the picturesque market square in the heart of the old town. The renaissance houses seemed impossibly perfect. When I mentioned this to my students the following week they laughed with gloomy satisfaction. Did Westerners not know any history? Most of Warsaw had been completely destroyed during World War II. The old town was just a faithful replica. As we sat in the square I started to feel slightly proprietorial about Sarah and Tashka and to enjoy the novelty of being Richard's understudy in matters such as folding the pushchair.

Later, when we met up with Richard at the British Council Library, he looked unusually animated. A day in the library – his natural habitat, I suspected – had clearly been a tonic from parenthood in a cramped flat, and he was looking very pleased with himself.

On Monday morning I set about teaching *writing* in a new way. A system of short individual tutorials seemed the best way for me to avoid the pitfalls of teaching the whole group. The students were more than happy to swap an hour and a half class for a ten minute slot every second week and besides were so used to doing what they were told there was never going to be any argument. There was none of the appearance of civilised equality enjoyed at British universities. Students required the signatures of all their teachers at the end of the academic year and knew that they could fail on the whim of any one of them. Most feared was Professor Zielińska, closely followed by Mr Krzeszewski, who enjoyed torturing his students with improbable vocabulary tests on things like *English plants and herbs* or *military ranks and weaponry*. By comparison the native speakers were pushovers. Nobody knew this better than Jacek, or Jack as he preferred to be known, and I came to dread our fortnightly conversation. Jacek signalled his disdain by swearing in English at every opportunity. His favourite word was 'fuck' which he combined variously with 'man' and 'hey'.

'Adam – I can call you Adam, right? – would you like to drink beer with some Polish men?'

'Jacek, have you brought any work to show me?'

'Fuck! I just asked you if you wanted to have a party. Next week I will bring some work. Do you know PVC windows?'

'What?'

'You never heard of them. Fuck!'

'No, of course I've heard of them.'

'If you want to make money I will introduce you to Radek. He sells PVC windows. I am his translator. If you need to borrow money you can ask me.'

Most of the students, however, were rather more subdued. The most mournful of all was a girl from Latvia who had failed her examinations and was repeating the year.

'Adam, I must tell you, I have had a lot of difficulties at the university. I think this year will be better for me because my Polish has improved. Last year I was very homesick but I think I will be happier now. Latvia is a very poor country, which is why I am doing my studies in Poland, but it is not easy for me here.'

In common with the majority of the Polish students, the girl was less than enthusiastic about the west and convinced of its indifference. Until I arrived in Poland I hadn't even heard of Latvia or its neighbour Estonia so perhaps their attitude was understandable.

Among many of the female students I found nineteenth century Polish romanticism mixed with a kind of straight-laced hippy sensibility. Their summer holidays seemed to consist of 'going to the forest' or 'walking in the mountains' and gentle mockery was out of the question. When I had tried this in a tutorial with another girl called Aśka, she had looked at me with a tragic expression and said, very earnestly, 'Please don't laugh at me.'

In general this new system of tutorials worked well. The exception to this was Zbigniew with whom I found it almost impossible to communicate. In the end I had to re-schedule his tutorial to the end of the morning to allow us time for the exhausting business of understanding each other.

The Department of English Philology was only four years old. The original intake had been whittled down to what was now the small group of melancholy fourth year students to whom I taught conversation on Wednesday mornings. For elder statesmen they were particularly uncooperative. To be fair to them they had had plenty of time to tire of visiting native speakers. They had also been terrorised by my predecessor – a school mam-ish young English woman I'd spoken to before I left England. She had been quite snooty about the Polish students and described their approach to writing English as 'pouring jelly into a mould'. She had also used her signature to bully and cajole them.

From my conversations with Richard and Sarah I gathered that the thing to do was to photocopy an article from Newsweek, read it aloud and then launch them into a discussion on the issues it raised. The article I selected for the first class examined the events leading up to the collapse of Poland's communist government and seemed ideal. In fact it was greeted by an audible sigh and stony silence. Eventually it was broken by

Andrzej, the group's acknowledged leader.

'I am sorry but people in Poland don't care about these things. We are tired of talking about communism and the war. I am sorry.'

The following week, going too far the other way, I began with a musical quiz. I hoped it might expose musical differences and that conversation would follow quite naturally. When it didn't, I at least had a handout to fall back on – useful vocabulary/ terminology for talking about music. I had tried to include the most technical expressions I could think of – mainly words associated with classical music (adagio, allegro, andante, etc).

Andrzej adjusted his spectacles and then broke it to me as gently as he could. 'We have all of these words. They are Italian.'

Conversation with the second year students invariably returned to the awkward subject of the Second World War. Britain's 'betrayal' of the Poles was another reason to resent native speaker teachers like myself. Most of the students blamed Britain for abandoning Poland to the German invasion in 1939 and then to Stalin and communism in 1945. When I tried to suggest that this might be a rather harsh interpretation of the events one of the boys in the group lost his temper. What did I know of Polish history? Nothing. How then could I presume to talk about Poland? The students spoke wearily about their country's history and gave a fatalistic shrug of the shoulders if pressed for an opinion. All of the group had wartime anecdotes from their grandparents but were reluctant to share them. In the university library I came across an account of the city's occupation which described the murder of an elderly and greatly respected priest. The inhabitants of Toruń had been made to carry out repairs on the iron road bridge across the

Vistula. One day the priest fell into the river, exhausted by the hard work. Some of the other workers dived in to try and save him but an SS guard shot him as he was attempting to swim to the bank. The book – entitled The Nazi New Order In Poland – had been published in 1941 just as Hitler was launching his attack on the USSR and foresaw a miserable future in which the *'land which produced Copernicus and Chopin, Mme Curie, Mickiewicz and Rosa Luxemburg, is to become a community of dispossessed manual workers, a reservoir of slave labour for the Reich.'*

Chapter Three

Vodka / Fish / Correspondence / Mother

When Basia went to stay with her sister the following weekend Waldek held an impromptu party. Waldek and his brother were already drinking vodka when I arrived early on Saturday afternoon. With them was a girl called Beata, a student of Polish literature. She had frizzy auburn hair and she and Waldek were laughing hysterically together on the sofa. Waldek's younger brother, Peter or Piotr, was a film buff and wanted to talk to me about the films I had seen in England.

Later in the afternoon two more guests arrived. Waldek's sister and her friend were both smartly dressed women in their mid-thirties. They had dressed formally for the occasion but didn't seem to mind or notice that the rest of us were drunk and dishevelled. When somebody suggested dancing Waldek sprang into life, moving furniture and selecting music. Dancing in Poland was not what I was used to. Couples danced as partners in the old fashioned sense even when the music playing was Guns & Roses. Shuffling around from one foot to another was starting to catch on in the student clubs but was hardly an option in Waldek's salon. I made straight for Beata who I imagined would be the least technical of the three women. She was also by a considerable distance the least sober and hardly seemed to notice when I trod on her foot or when we collided with the other two couples. After the first dance Waldek suffered a relapse and sunk back into his sofa. He was soon joined there by his brother. Coming home from the university in the afternoons I had seen men in overalls blankly zigzagging their way home literally paralysed after an hour at the vodka. There was clearly no prospect of either brother dancing, only of my being rotated to partner the three women. Nor could there be any question of clowning around with Waldek's sister and her friend. The friend was a demure divorcee with an elegant figure and a string of pearls in the opening of her shiny black blouse. Over her shoulder as we slowly circled the improvised dance floor I could see Waldek and his brother asleep on the sofa.

Fortunately, when Waldek woke up he felt hungry and persuaded his sister and her friend to help him prepare supper. Finally liberated I slumped down on the sofa next to Beata. Without warning she pulled me closer and enclosed me in a passionate embrace. We remained entwined on the sofa as the others came in and out with plates of food for supper. They each gave me a knowing look that recalled the words of the melancholy engineer in the *stołówka*.

After supper Beata locked herself in Waldek's bathroom, and I decided to go in search of Aśka. Waldek was talking to her softly through the grill on the bathroom door as I tip-toed out of the apartment.

I found Aśka in *Morski,* a student bar five minutes from where Waldek and I lived. She was dancing and waved to me to join her.

'Where have you been?'

'At Waldek's. Why?'

'You look drunk. We'd better sit down. I've got a favour to ask you. Have you heard of the Theatre of Fish? They're English.'

'No.'

'They are coming to the university next week to perform. I am organising it. I was wondering if they could stay at your flat. It would be really very helpful.'

I went with Aśka to meet the Theatre of Fish when they arrived by train late on Wednesday evening. Aśka had met them in her hometown Koszalin where they lived and studied under a master of mime/absurdist theatre. The three men were dressed like tramps from a Samuel Becket play in threadbare student coats and Dr Marten-style boots. Two of them carried a trunk containing their costumes and props. Carol, the fourth member of the group, a slightly frumpy looking woman in her forties, appeared to have little in common with the other three, and tensions surfaced as soon as we were in the taxi.

'Just fuck off, Graham, and give me a cigarette.'

'Graham. Carol would like a cigarette.'

'I know she would, but she's not getting one.'

'Would you like me to give you a cigarette, Carol, or would you prefer one of Damien's?'

'Thank you, Peter.'

Despite the fact that he said very little, Peter seemed to be the group's spokesman and leader. Everything about him was massive. His lips and ears were thick and rubbery and his forehead reminded me of a Huron Red Indian. Although he didn't seem to have been drinking he smelt of wine and his face was reddened by alcohol.

The group sat round my kitchen table chain smoking whilst Aśka and I made tea. Only Graham and Carol made any effort at conversation. Damien was busy rolling cigarettes for the others and Peter sat cocooned in a world of his own looking spaced out. After her cup of tea Carol was ready for bed and went off with Aśka to the student hostel.

After much more smoking the others agreed to retire for bed. I had no beds or bedding to offer them but they all seemed happy to sleep on the floor in their coats. In the morning I found Peter curled up in the hall next to the front door like a giant draught excluder.

I arrived early for the performance that evening intending offering my services on the door or backstage. Aśka was busy with some other students organising the door/box office and there didn't appear to be a backstage – the four members of Fish were already dotted around the improvised auditorium dressed in white shirts and dinner jackets and heavily made-up. I went over to talk to Graham but he just ignored me and continued pacing up and down. This was a bit rich I thought given my hospitality the previous evening. When I tried again, this time rather sarcastically, Graham snapped out of his pre-performance trance and turned on me impatiently.

'Look don't take this personally, OK, but I am psyching myself up. I don't talk to people before a show. I'll talk to you later.'

Reluctantly, I had to admit that Graham and the rest of Fish clearly knew what they were doing. Transformed in her black trouser suit, Carol was especially energetic and unrecognisable from the bad tempered woman who had arrived the night before. Even though many of the audience couldn't have followed the text, they were extremely appreciative and after the performance Fish enjoyed an evening of star status in the student bar.

There was some sort of 'freshers' event or initiation being held in the bar for the new students of English. Waldek and some of the other Polish teachers were there and when I sat down next to Aśka I noticed Mr Krzeszewski eying us beadily.

Carol had grumbled about sharing a room the previous evening and when she announced early that she was going to bed made it quite clear she didn't want to be disturbed. Rather than face Carol, at the end of the evening Aśka opted to stay at my flat with the other members of Fish. When she suggested sharing the bed I pretended not to have even considered it and curled up under my coat alongside Peter, Graham and Damien on the floor. The next day when they had gone I opened all the windows but the smell of smoke lingered on through the following week.

Aśka and I met for a drink that evening to celebrate their departure and believing that our dealings with Fish had put things between us on a more intimate footing, I tried to kiss her at a pedestrian crossing on our way back from town.

Under communism nobody crossed at a pedestrian crossing until the green man was showing. Even late at night when the streets were deserted – as on this occasion – local people waited patiently until the lights changed. Trying to steal a kiss as we waited didn't go down at all well. Aśka immediately pulled away and looked horrified. Equally horrified I fumbled an apology and when the lights finally changed we walked on in embarrassed silence.

This setback was immediately followed by Poland's national day of mourning – All Saints' Day on 1st November. The university closed and most students travelled back to their families. In the afternoon I went for a walk and ended up following my neighbours to the local cemetery. It was full of families tidying up the graves of their parents and grandparents. People swept the marble stones and laid fresh flowers and re-lit candles in an atmosphere of neighbourly good humour, smoking and sharing coffee from thermos flasks. Feeling like a total alien I hurried back to my flat and sat down and wrote a succession of plaintive letters home.

Later on, to cheer myself up, I went to see Waldek. Having decided that it was finally time to get my hair cut, I needed his advice.

'You know Adam, when you go to the hairdressers in Poland you must be careful. I don't trust them actually.'

'What do you mean?'

'There is a friend of Basia's who comes to the flat and cuts our hair. I think this is much safer.'

'Waldek, what are you talking about?'

'AIDS. I always make sure I am the first customer in the day if I go to the hairdressers. Then I know they are using a new razor.'

'How do you know that?'

'Basia's friend told me. Even if there is blood on it they just wipe it off. It is very unhygienic. But they use a new blade every day, so if you go when they've just opened you should be OK.'

Matters of health invariably brought out the Poles' natural pessimism. Aśka, for example, seemed to believe a story she'd heard about Polish drug addicts deliberately passing on the AIDS virus, attacking people with syringes on trains and buses. This was just the sort of story to get the other students nodding in agreement during conversation classes. The local doctors tended to prescribe handfuls of tablets for even the mildest ailment. Waldek, however, preferred to trust his own instincts whenever he was unwell. Hangovers were the work of 'toxins' in the water or blamed on the fact that the beer wasn't 'fresh'. He sometimes talked positively of riding a bicycle or doing 'gymnastics' on his balcony but nothing ever came of it.

On Saturday, meanwhile, my mother arrived bringing with her four Sainsbury's baking potatoes and the mixture for a rhubarb crumble.

In Kieślowski's film *Three Colours White* a group of customs men at Warsaw airport steal a heavy leather trunk belonging to a Polish Airlines passenger. They drive out to a patch of wasteland to inspect the contents only to find that the trunk contains a man, whom they then beat up for having wasted their time. Had customs picked on my mother's luggage, what would have been their reaction, I wonder, to four potatoes and a bag of uncooked crumble?

When I arrived in Warsaw on Saturday morning I took a taxi to the airport. Warsaw airport was supposed to be a bit of a dump so I wasn't too surprised when the taxi dropped me off outside some low wooden buildings on the edge of a forest. Inside I went in search of a snack and found a depressing canteen where women were dishing out various types of stew from industrial-sized saucepans. There were also the hunks of steaming boiled chicken and knuckles of pork I had seen people in Toruń tucking into for elevenses. I found this quite a disturbing sight until someone explained that the Polish working day was not nine to five as I had imagined; diners at the *Garmażeria*, where Richard and I went for morning coffee, had in fact probably been at work since seven am and were actually eating their lunch. The boiled meat never became any more appealing, but when the *Garmażeria* started selling ready roasted chickens I eagerly joined the long queue and began rehearsing the Polish for 'one roast chicken please', only to reach the counter and ask instead for '*jeden raz kurwa proszę*' – Polish for 'one prostitute please'.

However, it did strike me as odd sort of fair for an international airport to be serving. I also began to notice that every one in the airport building looked and seemed to be speaking Polish. When I checked the arrivals board there were no details of any flights from Heathrow or anywhere else I recognised. This terminal, they informed me at the information desk, was for domestic flights only.

My taxi was still in the lay-by outside. When I got back in and asked the driver to take me to the other terminal he just nodded deviously and pointed at the price on the metre.

Passengers from London had the choice of one flight a week to Warsaw – arriving Saturday afternoon and returning the following Saturday. By the time my mother's plane landed at half past two it was starting to get cold and evening was already beginning to draw in. We caught a bus back to the station and before boarding our train had a meal in the station restaurant. Soon to be replaced by fast food bars in the squalor of the huge booking hall, it bore all the hallmarks of communist customer service. First you were obliged to give up your bag and coat to the surly women in slippers manning the cloakroom; then, if you were lucky, one of the waitresses might acknowledge your arrival, and – always avoiding eye contact – eventually come over and serve you. Laughing self-deprecatingly as you stumbled through your order met with a bored look and an impatient snap of the menu as the waitress turned heel and went back to talking with her colleagues. When it came, the food, however, was always good and amazingly cheap. The wooden panels and plastic flowers also offered a little respite from the more monstrous ugliness of the rest of the station and its population of pickpockets and Romanian gypsies. Warsaw Central was a typically sympathetic piece of communist architecture built in the shape of a World War I tank. The platforms were down in the dark bowels of the station surrounded by iron girders and steel cables. As we waited for our train what looked like a military train pulled into the station. It was an overnight train from Moscow. A few bleary eyed passengers pulled back curtains and stared back at us from their unlit compartments but nobody left the train.

For Waldek my mother's arrival was a cause for celebration.

'Your mother is coming to Poland! You must feel very emotional. Come on! This is so English. I am sure she must be a wonderful woman. We must drink to your mother.'

I couldn't admit it to Waldek but there was one aspect of my mother's visit which made me feel a little uneasy. Since leaving England I had not telephoned any of my friends or family preferring instead to keep in touch by letter. I hadn't managed to make even a local call from the pay phones at the post office, so this was partly a matter of necessity; but I also rather liked the idea of Polish exile – toughing it out alone in a far away country etc. None of this, I realised, would be enhanced by having my mother come to stay. It had, as Sarah pointed out rather scornfully, only been six weeks since I'd left England.

Exile was all very well but only appealing so long as I was receiving regular news from home. Alistair wrote to tell me that Alan's sun bed empire had folded and that anybody who was anybody from university was now living in London, in case I was still planning my escape.

My parents sent a recording of Gary Lineker's appearance on *Desert Island Discs*. The interview was not exactly riveting but it made a pleasant change from fiddling with the reception on the World Service. The selection of music (GL: *'I am not the greatest music lover in the world. I like what I like…'*) was entirely predictable and could have belonged to any 1980s' footballer – Elton John, Rod Stewart, Eric Clapton, U2, Dire Straits, Simply Red etc. The whole thing seemed rather heavy going for the presenter Sue Lawley and contained no hint of the slick presenter of *Match of the Day*.

SL: *You sound all in all, I must say, rather saint-like. Very level headed. You've never been booked. You're happily married. You hardly drink. You don't go out much.*

GL: *Well, we go out quite a bit. To restaurants and things. I do like a glass of wine.*

SL: *But you're a good clean lad. Is there a great hall of indiscipline inside you which would like to break out?*

GL: *Basically, I am pretty boring really. I enjoy going out for a meal with my wife…*

Even the smallest package had to be collected from the post office. When I went to collect my first parcel I queued up at three different counters only eventually to find that a girl from Leicester had sent me a chocolate Wagon Wheel.

When I took my mother to meet Waldek I was relieved that he didn't try to kiss her hand as I had seen him do with other women but in other respects his behaviour was predictably chivalrous. I was demoted to the sofa next to him and my mother was placed in the special visitor's chair. He then served afternoon tea in a fine china tea service before addressing himself to the problem of what my mother would be doing whilst I was teaching. He should consider it an honour to act as her guide. Before we left Waldek requested that my mother play something on the piano and summoned Basia and his daughter Emilia to listen.

As well as Waldek, my mother also met Richard and Sarah. At their suggestion I invited them for dinner and my mother soon found herself being politely grilled (or 'Ruffed-up' as Sarah referred to it). What were the British press saying about Thatcher? Was she on the way out? Had she met Aśka? (I hadn't been totally honest with them about my lack of progress.) Would she mind taking back some small parcels/Christmas presents, and so on until, eventually, after desert (rhubarb crumble), Tashka woke up and demanded to be taken home.

Chapter Four

Aśka / Bydgoszcz / Christmas Shopping / Bartek

For a couple of weeks I saw virtually nothing of Aśka but the following Saturday afternoon, after my mother had left for Warsaw for her flight home, she came to my flat. Could she use my kitchen to prepare a cake? Her boyfriend had returned and was staying with her over the weekend. This wasn't great news but at least she'd left him behind in the student hostel.

As she didn't appear to want me hovering in the kitchen, and as I was determined not to appear too interested I sat in my living room listening to the football reports on the World Service. Later when I tried the cake mixture I was deliberately unenthusiastic.

Did her boyfriend not mind being left on his own, I asked, but Aśka just shrugged her shoulders. I wondered whether this apparent indifference was for my benefit or whether it was just the frostiness I was starting to expect from Polish women. As further proof of my disinterestedness I suggested meeting up with them in the evening for a drink but Aśka declined and hurried away rather sheepishly with her cake.

Instead I spent the evening at Waldek's. He and Basia

were entertaining friends for dinner – a young couple who were doctors – and he insisted I join them, although Basia, I was starting to suspect, could have done without me being around for one evening. Neither spoke any English. After a while Waldek stopped translating their horror stories from the operating theatre and I was happy to withdraw from the conversation and concentrate on looking politely agreeable whilst Waldek plied me with vodka. Eventually, unable to take any more Polish for one night, I excused myself and returned rather sulkily to my flat.

Only after consuming a much larger quantity of vodka would I again pluck up the courage to try anything with Aśka. On previous meetings it had invariably taken a couple of bottles of beer to overcome the chill factor/language barrier. I had grown used to long gaps in the conversation at the start of the evening, knowing that salvation was at hand. On one occasion, after a particularly awkward pause, I sighed *'Ho hum'*, simply meaning 'Here we go again' but the effect on Aśka was dramatic. She coloured deeply and began fidgeting uncomfortably in her seat, believing, it transpired, that I had just declared my love. Without realising it I had just told her that I loved her in Polish (*ho hum* sounds similar to *kocham*). Once this mistake was discovered I tried rather unconvincingly to laugh it off. How silly. Had she really not heard the expression 'ho hum'? However, I didn't want to back-pedal too far in case I killed off any notion of romance between us so I quickly changed the subject.

Eventually, at the end of an evening in November, Aśka agreed to come up to my flat for a nightcap. Forty-five minutes and a bottle of vodka later, we had kissed briefly and then fallen asleep on the floor where we sat. Aśka awoke in the morning to find me installed in the bathroom unable to utter a syllable. Very charitably, and apparently in reasonable health, she went in search of medicine and returned with an array of enormous tablets. Tactfully she then left me to the safety of my bathroom and the wave of nausea threatening to overwhelm me.

Luckily I was to be handed a reprieve in the form of an invitation to supper the following day, which consolidated the brief embrace of the previous evening and to my considerable relief, Aśka generally avoided coming to my classes thereafter.

Anxious to impress her with my spending power – I still had some of my original £150 left – I took Aśka to dinner at the Orbis Hotel. The various people from whom I'd sought advice all agreed that this was the best restaurant in Toruń. In fact the experience felt similar to visiting a Bernie Inn in England in the seventies, but without the prawn cocktail and the cheery service. Orbis was the old state owned tourist agency, responsible for holidays, buses and hotels – Polish communism's ministry of fun. The hotels were mainly for the benefit of foreign visitors. Waldek told stories of rooms being bugged by the Secret Police and had prepared me for the tepid reception from our tired looking waiter and the heavy square furniture of the empty dining room.

In the absence of a wine list we drank bottles of beer and after bowls of goulash soup ate beefsteak served with chips and grated vegetables. A hearty meal but not quite the cosmopolitan menu or ambience I had been hoping for.

When I paid the bill I made the mistake of saying 'Thank you very much' to the waiter. He took this as his cue to abscond with my change – nearly 100,000 złoty, almost half a week's wages. Fortunately I had Aśka with me. When the waiter didn't re-appear she was furious and went off to find him. She returned some time later with the money, full of indignation.

'Bloody cheek they have. They wouldn't dream of doing that normally. It's just because you're a foreigner.'

In the evenings, sat by the window in my kitchen, I started to look out for her as she crossed the tramline on her way to my flat, always carrying the leather satchel which she wore pinned across her blue coat like a postman. Now that there was no need to drink, and with temperatures outside plummeting, we stayed in and watched British and US TV series like *Dynasty* and *Capital City*. Fortunately there was no proper dubbing, just what sounded like the same man talking in Polish over the voices of the actors, and so it was still possible to make out what was being said.

Every so often normal lessons were cancelled because of a visit by a foreign academic. On these occasions the students filed dutifully into the grand seminar room to listen to a paper on the visitor's specialist subject. Richard seemed to particularly enjoy these occasions, providing as they did a rare opportunity for him to clash with other academics. One of the more contentious was the visit of a West German feminist whose topic was the *masculinisation of public buildings*. Her talk was accompanied by a series of slides showing empty corridors, stairwells and doorways.

'This corridor you see is totally masculine – aggressive straight lines, cold neutral colours and the environment is entirely sterile. It is devoid of nice feelings. At my university we have tried to improve this environment. Here you see the corridor has been updated to include a feminist perspective.

We have introduced potted plants, lots of round shapes and painted the walls orange. The doors have been left open.'

When Richard tried to interrupt ('I am sorry Sarah, but I find your argument quite offensive – ') he found his way barred.

'Richard, at my university we have tried to move away from this way of talking. We try to be more considerate and less violent. It is very masculine to interrupt other people.'

A more popular visitor was Jacques, a Professor of British History from Angers in France. In his analysis of Britain's frosty relations with its EU partners he identified Michael Haseltine as a possible saviour of Britain's good name. None of the students had ever heard of Michael Haseltine but this didn't deter Richard from pursuing the point – 'You say, Jacques, that you don't trust Thatcher. I am sorry but I don't trust Haseltine either...' He accepted Richard's intervention with a Gallic shrug of the shoulders whilst the students looked on nonplussed.

One morning towards the end of November the department's secretary appeared at my door whilst I was teaching, waving frantically for me to follow her. There was a telephone call for me in the office. It was my mother. Would I like her to book me a flight home for my Christmas present? She had got the number of a woman who specialised in travel to Poland but it would mean going to the LOT (Polish Airlines) office in Bydgoszcz to pick up my ticket.

This, I knew, was where the majority of my colleagues lived. Only Waldek and Mr Krzeszewski, of the Polish members of the department, lived in Toruń. When I mentioned to Ewa – the most friendly of the female teachers – that I would be coming to Bydgoszcz, she invited me for tea. She gave me her card and suggested I show it to the taxi driver when I arrived at the station.

Bydgoszcz was a larger and less attractive city than Toruń. After about an hour the train started to stop at short intervals, at stations all confusingly called Bydgoszcz. They serviced the depressing outskirts of the city – an Orwellian landscape of grey apartment blocks separated by patches of muddy grass sodden under a dirty layer of snow and ice. As if to underline the miserable uniformity, on the side of the buildings, daubed in enormous figures, was the number of each block – *68, 89,* and on up to *374* etc. It was to one such block, apparently in the middle of nowhere, that the taxi driver delivered me when I showed him Ewa's card. He didn't hang around to see if I had got the right address but sped off into the enveloping blizzard. I hurried across the permafrost to the shelter of the porch at the base of what was supposed to be Ewa's block and began pressing the buttons on the intercom. Eventually someone answered and let me in and I made my way to Ewa's door. Nobody answered, so I settled down on the stairs to wait for her to return.

After a while an elderly couple passed me on their way out. The sound of them unlocking the main door and of it clunking shut behind them echoed up the stair well. I was locked in. In the unlikely event of Ewa returning I wrote her a note and then moved downstairs to the hallway, ready in case someone opened the door. Eventually a little girl carrying vegetables let me out and I trudged back towards the main road in search of a taxi. There wasn't time now to track down Ewa so I flapped my arms in imitation of an aircraft to indicate to the driver that he should take me to the LOT office.

There would be no time when I returned to England to do any Christmas shopping so I had to set about it before I left.

Money was also an issue and made it absolutely necessary to buy Polish. Foreign teachers were paid a *Senior Lecturer's* salary – about one and a half million złoty a month, which worked out as about £90 a month and falling. By the summer the value of the złoty in relation to sterling had more than halved.

The local shops were not exactly stacked with potential Christmas presents. The state souvenir shops (*Cepelia*) specialised in peasant costumes and handicraft. There were only so many small painted wooden boxes one could buy so I fell back on local staples like flavoured vodka and candles. The candles seemed particularly good value but were in fact intended to be used for gravestones, a *faux pas* which only became apparent on Christmas Day when one of the lucky recipients (unfortunately an elderly relative) lit one of them indoors, releasing a plume of black smoke. Equally unsuccessful was the ginger bread frieze of the old town I bought for my grandmother, who wasn't sure whether to eat it or put it on the wall but I suspect probably threw it away as soon as she got home.

To mark the end of term the Teacher Training College at which Waldek and Mr Krzeszewski also taught were throwing a Christmas party. Mercy Schwimmer was there wearing a long black skirt, greeting people as they arrived – 'Waldek. How are you?' and to Aśka and myself, 'You guys are together. Neat.' Piotrek, now Mercy's fiancé, had his arm round her and was grinning. All of the other students present were smartly dressed young women, to whom I had often heard Waldek refer rather lecherously as the 'girls from the college'. He had brought Bartek from the department along with him, who, as usual, looked slightly awkward and said very little. Later, when the whole party had removed to a nearby student bar, Bartek asked me if he could stay with me for the night as he had missed his train home to Bydgoszcz.

The prospect of topping and tailing with Bartek was not an appealing one. I had barely exchanged more than a few words with him during the course of the term, and besides he was extremely big. Aśka, as usual, had the solution. The two girls who shared her room in the student hostel were away. I could stay with her and Bartek could have my little sofa bed to himself. Waldek could let him into the flat and I could collect the keys from him in the morning. I thought no more about it.

I certainly wasn't prepared for the macabre scene which greeted us when we returned the following morning. A trail of tomato puree, which began at the fridge, led across the kitchen floor and up the wall. A roast chicken had vanished from the fridge; only a few small bones remained and a broken knife lay on the plate amongst the debris. A bottle of red wine lay on its side in the lounge and much of its contents had been spilt. In the circumstances I wasn't particularly surprised to find that the bed had not been made but nevertheless stored it up with my other grievances. Aśka and I nervously checked the cupboards expecting to find a dead body and then set about cleaning up.

Waldek was uncharacteristically shifty when I confronted him about this later in the day.

'Waldek, he ate a whole chicken. The bones as well. The man's an animal.'

'Oh dear. I am sorry, Adam.'

'Why are you sorry? It's not your fault.'

'I think we drank your wine as well.'

'We?'

'Oh dear.'

'I don't blame you Waldek but why didn't he clean up in the morning or leave a note.'

'He was probably embarrassed.'

I couldn't argue with this but decided I would ignore Bartek until he saw fit to apologise. Weeks later, by which time my coolness had become obvious even to Bartek, he bashfully raised the subject of the chicken and the air was cleared.

On the last day of term our secretary handed me a yellow hand towel and a bar of soap. She couldn't speak any English but smiled encouragingly so I took it and smiled back. When I showed it to Marek the librarian he opened one of the drawers of his desk and produced an identical towel.

'It is from the Rector. It's a present,' he chuckled.

It was our Christmas bonus.

That evening Waldek drove me to the station. In the waiting room old women huddled for warmth surrounded by their bundles. Men lay curled up asleep on the wooden benches. Since I'd last been there some attempt had been made to brighten the place up – a small kiosk was selling food and drinks and there were posters of Samantha Fox and Sabrina on the wall.

Although infrequent, Polish trains ran through the night, and even though it was around midnight when I boarded the train it was full of people – students travelling home with their rucksacks for Christmas, young army conscripts in their green First World War uniforms, tired looking men with moustaches, and women wrapped up in thick coats wearing lots of make-up. Later, when I changed trains and joined an express to Warsaw, there were no seats free so I stood, guarding my rucksack anxiously whilst a drunk lurched up and down the corridor. He was a good deal taken by my bag and observed it enviously as if he knew I was taking vodka home for Christmas.

Chapter Five

Interlude / Winter / Alistair / Gdańsk /
Kraków / Koszalin

Alistair had been right. Most of my friends, it seemed, were living in a large house in Finchley. Alistair had now got a proper job but Alan's sun bed business had ended in acrimony with him owing money and, fearing reprisals, refusing to answer the door. I had also missed the arrival of The Stone Roses, Star Burger restaurants, and Gascoigne's magical spell of form for Tottenham; but Poland hadn't been the disaster my friends had predicted and there was no question now of not going back.

Before I returned I withdrew the last of my savings from the building society to buy a guitar and presents for Aśka. On the flight back to Warsaw I had to hand over the guitar to one of the flight attendants who ferried it away for safekeeping. Towards the end of the flight she came to me and whispered, 'I've lost your instrument', and gestured to me to follow her. She had put it in one of the empty seats at the back of the plane but there was now no sign of it. Only when we landed was it discovered, having been buried under a pile of leather coats belonging to a large German man.

Hanging around Warsaw station with my guitar case and the rest of my luggage, I imagined myself easy prey for the pickpockets and couldn't relax until I was on the train back to Toruń.

Poland was several degrees colder when I returned in January. The women selling radishes at the roadside had disappeared and so too the fruit and vegetable stall outside by the tram stop. In fact fruit and vegetables seemed to have disappeared altogether and there were long queues just to buy onions and potatoes. My bath taps had started emitting muddy brown water but otherwise everything else just about continued to function despite the heavy snow falls.

Back at the university, Zbigniew, one of my first year Writing students, told me about the trouble his father had had at Christmas with the carp – their traditional supper. It was customary to buy the carp still alive and keep it swimming around in the bath until the man of the house killed it on Christmas Eve. As an alternative to clubbing the carp to death in the bath – the traditional method – his scientist father had rigged up an electric element, hoping to avoid this traumatic annual encounter. Unfortunately, the poor fish was left thrashing around noisily as it slowly boiled to death, much to the distress of the whole family.

Jacek didn't show his face until the third week of term. He'd been abroad on a business trip with Radek as his interpreter. Radek was now importing Spanish chocolate and had just bought a new car from the profits.

'What car do you drive in England?'

'Why do you want to know that?'

'Radek has just bought a new Renault. Yesterday we drove

to Poznań. Two hundred kilometres in two hours.'

'My father has a Ford Orion.'

'I am going to buy a Volkswagen. Radek will lend me some money. Would you like me to bring you some chocolate next week?'

The English Department had also come into some money via an EU scheme called the Tempus project. There were two new computers and a photocopier and also money to pay for an exchange programme with Keele University and the University of Angers in France. A delegation from Angers would be visiting Toruń at the start of the February vacation and Waldek was already busy preparing for their reception.

As usual Professor Zielińska had left all the donkey work to Waldek and Mr Krzeszewski.

'You should hear how this bloody woman speaks to me! We must hold a party, Waldek. Can I leave this to you and Krzysztof to organise? I will be in Warsaw when they arrive but I will be able to come to the party. Really I don't mind looking after them but the way she speaks to me is terrible. Waldemar, we can hold the party at your flat. Will it be big enough do you think? Professor Pawlik would never say this.'

The uncomfortable stand-off with my fourth year Conversation class was brought to an end in January with their departure to Keele as part of the exchange programme. Instead I was asked to teach conversation to Aśka's Texts' class. With very little difficulty Aśka persuaded me to let her and subsequently some of the other students organise the lessons for me. The first of these was a marked improvement on previous Conversation classes and established the start of an increasingly informal arrangement. After a few weeks the group decided to hold the class in the snack bar in the basement, reducing my role to tea-drinking spectator.

Alistair had promised to visit in the New Year and wrote to confirm his arrival at the start of the February holiday.

Will arrive in Warsaw in two weeks from this Saturday. Expect to be met and introduced to any reasonably attractive female students. I am doing my best not to think about sex as it occupies too much of my time and depresses me too much; I am strongly considering either going celibate or gay – either way would probably cause less problems. George Michael seems to have conquered both markets – I have recently purchased another of his albums to add to my rapidly growing CD collection. I may well take the opportunity in Poland to purchase a ready-made classical collection – what do you think the quality is like. Are they made in Poland or somewhere decent?

Up yours, Al

Towards the end of January Sarah made good on her promise of a Sunday roast. Before lunch Richard and I went with Tashka to a park next to the city zoo. It was clear and very cold and even though we were bathed in sunshine the snow was frozen hard. In their cages the animals walked around stoically trying to keep warm. Over lunch we discussed Richard's Christmas present for Sarah – a novel about the complicated love affairs between a group of university academics. I hadn't heard of it before so Richard gave me a detailed account of the characters and plot and after that we talked about his PhD thesis. He was returning to England for his viva at the end of the month and had been busy going over the proofs.

A few weeks later I came home to find a note from Richard pushed under my door – inviting me to join him for dinner, and signed 'Dr Ruff'. Over dinner he told me about his visit to Professor Zielińska. She lived in a large house on the outskirts of Warsaw and he had spent the night there before catching his flight to London. Richard had bravely challenged her about her imperious way of dealing with the students and she had reacted quite badly. Until then Richard had been Professor Zielińska's favourite, but she was more wary of him from then on.

This didn't prevent Richard from pushing through his pet project – the re-organisation of the department's library. Although Marek, the librarian, had everything catalogued on index cards, books were arranged on the shelves in what appeared to be completely random order. Taking a book out was rather like shopping only even slower; having placed your order there was usually a short delay of a few minutes whilst Marek searched for a pencil so that he could write it down, and then a much longer wait as he disappeared behind the shelves to look for your books. According to Waldek ('he's a very good chap') Marek was a great improvement on his predecessor and had inherited much of the muddle. He had been responsible for the introduction of index cards but what Richard was planning seemed to come as a bit of a shock. He puffed out his cheeks and sank bank into his chair as if he were about to hand over the keys to his house. Richard wasn't going to give up and at the end of term assembled some of the staff and a few of the older students to help him with the grand re-organisation. Marek looked on anxiously and somewhat bemused, like an elderly man having his bungalow refurbished by a team of decorators.

Alistair arrived in Warsaw the following Saturday wearing only a thick checked shirt and a woolly cardigan against the Polish winter. On the bus to the station he told me about his visit to Becksy – the pup he had brought to live with us in Leicester. A new home had been found for him with a firm of butchers. Even though the dog was being thoroughly spoiled it had been a difficult visit. Fiona, his girlfriend, had cried in the car on their way home and he clearly felt a bit guilty about the whole episode.

There was no vegetarian option for Alistair at the station restaurant so we both had the fried chicken and boiled vegetables before catching the train back to Toruń.

Later we met Aśka and some of her friends in one of the student bars. Jacek was also there and made a beeline for Alistair. When he started bragging about business opportunities in Poland, Alistair produced his smart new business card. Unfortunately, Jacek was impressed and arranged another meeting the following evening.

I had discouraged Alistair from bringing too much money with him and he had taken me at my word, arriving with only £50. Although this represented half a typical month's salary it wasn't quite as much as my letters may have suggested and I had to intervene towards the end of the evening to dissuade him from offering to buy everyone else in the bar a drink.

The next morning we sat in my kitchen eating our way through a loaf of fresh bread with strawberry jam and watched the people passing below. I was anxious to know what he'd made of Aśka.

'She's obviously reasonably bright but I wouldn't like to get on the wrong side of her.'

'Why do you say that?'

'Don't you think she's a bit scary?'

'I know what you mean.'

I recounted the occasion of our first row; when I had playfully pushed Aśka backwards over a low wall on which we were sat into a bed of shrubs.

'Yes, I could see that not going down very well. What did she do?'

'Sulked for ages.'

'Well that's women for you. Her friend was nice. What's her name?'

'Aska.'

Jacek called for us at my flat the following evening having promised to take us to his favourite bar. It turned out to be in a dark basement. Behind the bar cans of imported Heineken – sold at five times the price of a bottle of Polish beer – were stacked precariously in elaborately constructed pyramids. Jacek insisted on buying all the drinks and seemed a bit put out when we ordered Polish beer in preference to Heineken. We sat in one of the dimly lit alcoves and listened politely to Jacek's drinking stories.

'If you want we can drink vodka tonight Radek will be at the Hotel Orbis later on. If you are with me this won't be a problem. Maybe you want to meet hookers? I can arrange this for you.'

In fact we were planning an early night before catching a train to Gdańsk the following morning.

'I will drive you to Gdańsk. Radek will let me use his car and we can have a party tonight.'

In an attempt to put him off I reminded him rather pompously that he was my student and that technically I was his teacher. It might be awkward if we seemed to be too friendly.

'Bullshit. What about you and Asia? I am sorry to say it but none of the teachers at the university know what they are doing. The Polish teachers don't give a shit about us. I got drunk before my entrance exams and they still let me in. They don't care what the native speakers do.'

From the railway station in Gdańsk we went in search of the famous shipyard gates which Lech Wałęsa had scaled during the *Solidarity* strikes ten years before. A bitingly cold wind blew through the shipyards from the Baltic Sea and after posing for photographs next to the *Solidarity* monument we scurried off towards the old town in search of cover. Alistair spotted a red and white *Solidarity* umbrella in a shop window – a rash purchase he was starting to question even as we sat down for lunch – and decided it was the ideal present for his girlfriend Fiona.

Back out on the street after our lunch it was even colder and it was already starting to get dark as we trudged down the main street. It was flanked by tall Renaissance houses, which had been painstakingly reconstructed after the war, and led down to a gateway and a freezing harbour where the wind felt even colder. We hurried back up the street to the City Museum housed inside the Town Hall. Neither of us, however, were prepared to swap thick boots for little woollen slippers, as directed by the forbidding woman on the cloak room, and so found ourselves back out on the street in the cold, still with several hours to kill.

Someone was playing the organ in an enormous Gothic church just off the main street. Eventually we found the door and arrived in time to hear the last chord fading away. The white washed walls and draughty pews weren't exactly the pick-me-up we were looking for and so we headed back to a teashop we had seen earlier and stayed there until it was time to catch our train back to Toruń.

Polish railway carriages usually had the hot dry feel of a launderette with heat billowing up from beneath the seats. Not on this occasion, however. A thick layer of ice had formed inside the windows of the compartment. Even Alistair's ridiculous umbrella had ceased to be funny and most of the journey back passed in depressed silence.

The next day Waldek was having his party for the delegation from Angers. He and Basia were both dressed formally for the occasion – Waldek in a woollen waistcoat and cravat – and they both looked rather uncomfortable. They were still nervously awaiting the arrival of Professor Zielińska with the French party. Waldek hardly managed to smile even when we handed him a bag full of beer and when Richard and Sarah arrived with Tashka in her pushchair Basia shook her head disapprovingly. (Later in the year when I held a small dinner party for various members of the department, the first person to arrive was Sarah who immediately insisted on her and Tashka having a bath. Anyone who wanted the toilet just had to wait until Sarah finally emerged from the bathroom in a cloud of steam wearing my dressing gown.)

The French delegation consisted of three people, all teachers at the University of Angers – a heavily built elderly lady who spoke neither Polish or English; Monsieur Picot, a tall man with a high forehead and a very straight nose who was also wearing a cravat; and Alexandra, a Polish woman in her thirties who had emigrated to France.

Waldek served cheese and sausage on sticks with a choice of Bulgarian wine or vodka.

Next to the Polish women in our department Alexandra seemed very modern. She dressed and smoked with typical French poise and had shed the attitude of disapproving reticence which made some Polish women such hard work. She had grown up in Kraków, the ancient capital of Poland in the south of the country. It was the only medieval city left in Poland she said, and the most beautiful city in Europe, and we had to visit it before Alistair went back to England. I imagined something like the film sets in King Arthur films and promised her that we would go the following day.

Alistair, meanwhile, was enjoying the novelty of telling people about his new job. 'Working in London' sounded much more impressive than Leicester, even if his office was in fact in Watford.

Later on in the evening I found myself sharing the sofa with Professor Zielińska. Although her eyelashes fluttered and she laughed playfully there was no mistaking the cold edge in her voice.

'You must tell us whether you want to stay for another year or I will have to tell Aleksander (Professor Pawlik) to look for another native speaker whilst he's in America.'

Not knowing what to say I raised the problem of the exchange rate (i.e. earning about £90 a month) but to no avail.

'Oh dear. Really money isn't everything. And as far as I know you have no job in England but you have one here. I am sure your parents won't mind if you stay here for another year. Ah, there you are Małgorzata, come and sit here with us.'

I took this as my cue to leave and went off to fetch another drink. I found Waldek slicing cheese in the kitchen. He had cheered up considerably and had obviously been smoking out of the kitchen window.

'I must say, Professor Zielińska is not really a bad person. I shouldn't have said the bad things I said about her the other day. She can be very kind sometimes. She bought Basia some chocolates. Would you like one?'

The following morning Aśka quickly organised our train tickets and by lunchtime we were on our way to Kraków. The central part of Poland, to Warsaw and beyond, was unremittingly flat and there was little to see through the drizzle and dim afternoon light except thick forest. Only in Łódź, Poland's second largest city where Sarah had taught at the university, was there anything interesting to see – enormous red brick textile factories like those in Manchester, surrounded by railway tracks and pipelines. Stood forlornly in the middle of this were also blocks of flats built since the war. Sometimes giant oil or gas pipelines ran just in front of people's balconies on which they hung washing, smoked and kept their bicycles. It was a miserable scene - rusting machinery, broken window panes in dark factory buildings, long grass pushing up between the railway tracks – but every so often we passed plots of carefully tended allotments, speckled beneath a flurry of snow.

By the time we arrived in Kraków, around eight o'clock in the evening, the heavy snowfall was beginning to freeze. On Sarah's advice we headed for the *Dom Turysty* where we were greeted by a stern looking woman in a blue uniform.

'Passports.'

The woman looked up just once to check our likeness. Whilst she spoke she was busy preparing the official forms needed to register our stay.

'What is your occupation?'

'Teacher.'

'And yours?'

'Market research.'

She seemed particularly unimpressed by this and resumed even more briskly than before.

'This is your key. You must pay a deposit of ten thousand złoty in case you lose it. If you want breakfast you must pay extra, five thousand złoty. You must also pay for your room now. Please inform us of your departure a day before you wish to leave. Can you tell me for how many nights you wish to have the room?'

'Just tonight actually.'

'You must inform reception of this this evening. Enjoy your stay in Kraków.'

The *Dom Turysty* was at least close to the centre of the old town. The huge square and the famous Cloth Hall were only a few minutes walk away and looked spectacular glistening under the snow and ice. It was completely deserted and, absurdly, I felt as if we had stumbled on an unknown treasure. After a lap of the square and a drink in a cavernous student bar we went in search of food. All we could find was an expensive nightclub/ bar down a side street. Having paid the exorbitant entrance fee and the woman on the cloakroom, we sat down at one of the tables around a small dimly lit dance floor. Two men in white suits were setting up their instruments on a stage to our left.

The band struck up just as our food arrived. A dancer, draped in a black cloak, ran onto the dance floor and cavorted next to us, naked but for her cloak and a G-string.

'Oh my God! Don't look or she'll come over.'

We tried to avoid showing too much interest in the performance and got on with eating our chips. When she'd finished several smartly dressed couples made their way to the dance floor and danced elaborately to the accompaniment of the synthesiser and bass guitar. Feeling rather out of place and disgruntled at having paid the entrance fee we retrieved our coats and traipsed back to the *Dom Turysty* and our spongy iron beds.

Breakfast in the hotel's austere dining room consisted of a hard-boiled egg with a glass of black tea. Thus replenished we set off along the city wall in the direction of Wawel castle, the ancient seat of Polish kings, and also, bizarrely, one of the seven Hindu charkas – centres of exceptional supernatural energy. According to Hindu legend Lord Shiva threw seven magic stones towards seven parts of the world and one of them landed in Kraków. Along with Delhi, Delphi, Jerusalem, Mecca, Rome and Velehrad in the Czech Republic it was supposed to give off exceptional spiritual strength. Neither of us was at all conscious of this as we shuffled about in the snow trying to work the automatic timing device on Alistair's new camera. Later Alistair claimed that the cold had affected the camera, which was why everything looked as if it had been photographed in a tunnel.

The cold was also starting to affect us and after a quick look inside the Gothic cathedral – where Pope John Paul II had served as Poland's primate before his election – we made our way unsteadily down the other side of the hill on which both the cathedral and the castle stood and back towards the main square.

The Renaissance Cloth Hall was now open and as we passed through the covered arcade Alistair – probably the least tactile person I knew – found his arm grabbed by a small head-scarved woman holding a baby. She held out a piece of cardboard on which something was written in Polish, presumably asking for money. We immediately sped up but the woman held on to Alistair's arm and ran along beside us until we gave her some money. Immediately lots of other similarly dressed women also carrying babies flocked towards us from under the arches of the Hall.

Sympathetic souls like Jacek had told me a little bit about the Romanian gypsies in conversation classes. Their appearance in Polish cities had followed the overthrow of communist government in Romania and across the rest of Eastern Europe. According to Jacek the men folk were having a whale of a time drinking vodka in small secret dens on the outskirts of towns whilst their women and children walked the streets begging to pay for them. Later in the year when a small Romanian boy approached me for money in the main square in Toruń, remembering Jacek's stories, I bought him an ice cream instead. I took it over to where he was sitting with his mother on the steps of a church but the boy looked disgusted with my offering and let it drop on to the steps.

We hurried out of the Cloth Hall onto the square with the women in hot pursuit. Feeling harassed as well as cold and hungry we decided to have lunch in the first restaurant we came to. It was only midday and it was beginning to dawn on us that we still had twelve hours to fill until our train back to Warsaw with nothing very much to do. We had seen most of the sights and it was starting to get too cold for walking about. As if to remind us how slowly time was passing, every hour was announced by a trumpet call from the tower of the church in the main square.

We lingered over lunch for as long as we could and then went to a nearby cinema which was showing a Kim Bassinger film.

After the film we walked back to the *Dom Turysty* to pick up our bags and have a drink in the bar. In one corner three men were drinking vodka and coke and talking in raised voices. Two of them were obviously Poles – wiry and pale with bristly moustaches. Their companion, who was younger and smaller, was making most of the noise. I had noticed him turning round to look at us and after a while he came over to our table.

'You're speaking English right? Hey, Marek, these guys speak English!'

When his companions didn't react he shouted something to them in Polish but they just shrugged their shoulders and turned away.

'What are you guys doing here? You're English, right. This is incredible. I haven't spoken English in three months. I am staying south east of here with my uncle's family. My dad immigrated to Toronto in the sixties. I am Canadian. I'd never even heard of this place he's from. It's like a village in the middle of nowhere. That's where I am staying now. I've taken a year out of school to come and see my relatives. It's been amazing. The communists fucked everything up but Poland is such a great country and the girls here are really cute. They love anyone who's from Canada so I've had a lot of fun. Why don't you come over and meet my cousins?'

I made our excuses. We had to leave shortly to catch our train to Warsaw.

'You guys aren't very sociable. This is like the first chance I've gotten to speak English. You can talk to each other anytime.'

'I am sorry but we really have to go in a minute.'

'Great. Well, fuck you.'

He stomped off back to his seat.

Kraków had begun to lose its lustre. Our first sight of the city looking so magnificent the previous evening now seemed an awfully long time ago. Alistair was starting to wish himself back in Finchley and was growing anxious about getting to Warsaw in time for his flight home. Our train wasn't in fact due to leave for another five hours. I had lied to our Canadian friend and we still had a long wait ahead of us.

When it came our train was full of people returning from Zakopane – a ski resort in the Tatra Mountains. All of the compartments were full and the corridors were stuffed with luggage and skiing equipment. We found a small space to stand in and, because we had got on the wrong train, spent the next seven hours in grave discomfort fretting over our extremely slow progress.

Alistair just made it to the airport in time and seemed delighted to be going home. I caught the train back to Toruń and arrived home to find that the water had been turned off. I took my bucket to a pump Waldek had shown me beneath a neighbouring block of flats and got enough murky water for a cup of tea and an underarm wash before setting out once again for the railway station. I had arranged to visit Aśka at her parents' home in Koszalin up near the Baltic coast – a six hour journey involving three changes of train and another night in either very hot or very cold railway carriages.

Aśka's family lived in one of the many blocks of flats on the outskirts of Koszalin. One of the three small bedrooms was occupied by babcia – grandma. Amongst the diminutive forms of names used by the family was 'baboonia', an endearing form of grandmother, whilst Aśka was variously Joasiu, Aśku or Asieńko, and Aśka itself was a diminutive of Joanna.

Baboonia spent much of the day sitting in the tiny kitchen overseeing the preparation of food, a process which seemed to occupy most of the day. She herself seemed not to eat anything but hovered expectantly during meal times waiting for our verdict on the day's soup. She was especially interested in my opinion, eying me watchfully as I ate, and I was obliged to master a selection of effusive compliments – the Polish for 'that was very tasty' or 'that was delicious, grandma.' The compliment wasn't returned. When I cooked the family a curry Aśka's grandmother made a rare appearance at the dinner table to inspect my offering but required gentle persuasion and the addition of a lot of salt before continuing.

The lavish hospitality I enjoyed was offset by the trauma of going to the toilet and I avoided it at all costs. All of the rooms in the flat led off from a small central hallway, so that sat on the toilet one still felt very much at the centre of things. In the evenings when the family were at home it was impossible to go to the toilet without everyone knowing, and during the day Baboonia was only a few feet away on her perch in the kitchen. Later when she got a dog it would sniff inquisitively around the grill at the base of the toilet door whenever I was inside. The dread of letting out a huge fart at such close quarters haunted me. The toilet itself was no bigger than a telephone box. I was forced to sit as deep on the seat as I could and even then my knees were squeezed uncomfortably against the door. Rising from the toilet seat wasn't easy to do in such a confined space. If I leant forward too far I hit my head on the door, so I was forced to adopt the braced, straight-backed posture of a weight lifter.

Whenever I encountered Aśka's grandmother in the morning she looked at me as if I had just returned from the dead and the conversation followed what became a familiar pattern.

(Sarcastically) 'Did you get enough sleep?'

'Yes, thank you.'

(Pointedly) 'It was a long sleep.'

'Yes.'

(Wearily) 'Breakfast?'

'Yes, please.'

I was thankful that conversation could not go beyond these wary pleasantries. Aśka, I soon realised, had said very little to her parents about our relationship, and it was obvious that the family were watching our behaviour closely. When we visited Aśka's godmother she was similarly observant and rather less friendly and made several pointed remarks about the problems of understanding different cultures. Clearly suspicious of my motives, she could, unfortunately, also speak some English and ask awkward questions about what I was intending to do the following year.

The morning conversation with Aśka's grandmother usually took place at about half past eight by which time Aśka's parents had gone to work. Given the severity of the winter weather it seemed unnecessarily cruel to begin the working day at seven o'clock. Like building uncovered stadiums, I wondered if perhaps it was a communist ruse to prevent people from getting too comfortable. (Another was the compulsory swimming class Aśka had to attend on Friday mornings. Without the signature of the swimming instructor the university could fail her regardless of her academic performance. Amenable doctors might be persuaded to write a sick note, but otherwise students had no option but to attend.) But by four o'clock in the afternoon her parents were back at home sitting down to the main meal of the day and repeats of the American series Dynasty – and for me the novelty of Joan Collins speaking with the voice of a Polish man.

Chapter Six

Dutch Boys / Boyfriend Trouble / Easter

When I got back to Toruń Waldek took me to see his new den – a room in the student hostel which he'd converted into a study. His father had helped him install an enormous wooden desk on which were arranged, in neat piles, pens and paper and his books on linguistics. This was where he was planning to write his PhD, although there was no sign of any of his things having been touched.

'To tell you the truth, Adam, I have been too busy sorting out the room. And I have been writing postcards to some of my friends.'

Waldek seemed more excited about the installation of a telephone. 'Would you like to call somebody? Shall we ring my brother? He could join us here. Anyway, cheers.'

At the start of the new term I found that Jacek had been given his marching orders by Professor Zielińska. When I next came across him at a concert in one of the student bars he was predictably bullish about the whole episode – 'Hey, can I say this *'she can kiss my arse'*?' – and in fact seemed cockier than ever surrounded by his new friends – a group of Dutch marketing students. One of them stepped forward and introduced himself.

'Ayld. Hey.'

He had very long legs and a small head, like the cartoon character Tin Tin.

'Jack said you are from Great Britain.'

'Yes, that's right.'

'An English hooligan, like Paul Gascoigne?'

'I was Jacek's teacher at the university.'

'I know that. This was my joke. I always like to speak with English people because of their sense of humour.' Then he added, 'If you like to eat spicy food we are making a party at Jack's flat tomorrow. Raymond is cooking some hot chilli.'

When Jacek opened the door of his grandmother's flat the following evening, I noticed, to my surprise, that he was wearing a pair of slippers. Having made me leave my shoes at the front door he then offered me my own pair, before wandering back to the kitchen to trade insults with one of the Dutch boys.

Although the conversation invariably revolved around the group's sexual conquests the Dutch boys were a welcome addition. The following weekend they held a party at their student hostel for Queen Beatix's birthday. Their university teachers from the Hague were also there and sat on the floor cross-legged drinking cans of lager. One of them complimented me on my English. Later, having discovered that I was a native speaker, he suggested I help two of the group – Ruud and Raymond – with their final presentation which was to be delivered in English. They had been placed at a local bottle factory and asked to apply the modern marketing strategies they had learnt in Holland.

Later in the evening the party moved to one of the student bars and attracted the attention of a group of smartly dressed American evangelists. The Polish students appeared nonplussed by the approaches of men in suits offering Christianity and for the Americans it was a relief to find people speaking their language.

'Hey guys. It's really good to see you. Can we join you? This is John and I am Luke. We must look kinda odd to you but we're just going round talking to young people here about the Good News. We're having the most amazing experience. We thought there'd be like some hostility to us as Christians coming to a communist country but it hasn't been a problem. I guess it might be more difficult when we get to Russia but here the people seem real happy to talk about Jesus Christ.'

The Dutch – traditionally liberal and secular with a history of religious non-conformism – could hardly have been less fertile ground for right wing Christian evangelists – added to which most of the group were atheists. John and Luke grinned over their bibles and beer whilst one of the Dutch boys launched into an earnest critique of religious faith.

'This argument does not make sense. As we understand more about science it is not necessary to rely on religion so much. It is like with the sun. When we didn't know what it was we used to worship the sun but now we have electricity. Nobody worships the sun anymore. It is the same with Christianity. It is being replaced by science and medicine.'

Alistair wrote to tell me he had received a visit from Waldek, who was in England on a week's secondment at Keele University.

First of all, may I thank you for sending Waldek to visit me. I hope that I played my part as host adequately. He seemed to be very reticent to take anything off me, but I do realise that the value of the beer and the Chinese meal I bought him was about a week's salary for him. When he rang up during the week I told him to give me a ring at about 7 pm on the Sunday evening to arrange a meeting. He turned up at my house at about 3 pm in the afternoon while I was still psyching myself up for the event. This threw me greatly. He was incredibly attentive to Fiona and kept drawing her little pictures and teaching her to speak Polish. Just before he went to bed, he took me to one side and said that he wanted to give me a present that I could not refuse. Great, thinks me, vodka! Alas, a really lovely silver ashtray. I don't know if it showed but I really had trouble hiding my distaste. He was also seen late that night wandering about my house in his underpants, bedroom door open, revelling in the opulent western luxury.

It took me ages to recover from my trip. I was physically and mentally exhausted. When I got back it was even colder than in Poland. Minus 6 degrees at dinner time. The plane took five attempts to land due to snow and fog and some of the Poles were crying and praying etc., etc.

Waldek had taken Alistair a bottle of vodka but had drunk it himself during the week. He had picked up the ashtray at Victoria station in the buffet restaurant.

It wasn't long before Aśka and I went to Koszalin again. She had fallen over on a pedestrian crossing and sprained her wrist, so needed help carrying her bags. This time we were met by her father and as we squeezed into his little Fiat I noticed a man on the other side of the road watching us. Aśka, I could tell, had also seen him and began to get impatient with her father who was taking a long time to start the car. I realised, to my alarm, that this must be her jilted boyfriend.

As soon as we got to their flat Aśka disappeared for secretive talks with her parents. The ex, it transpired, had placed a personal ad in the local paper appealing for her return. Aśka's parents were anxious about how this might impact on her younger brother and asked her to go and speak to him. I accompanied her into town and then waited a safe distance from his flat whilst she went in to sort things out. After about an hour Aśka re-appeared with the ex by her side. They were heading straight for me, but, just as an unpleasant showdown seemed inevitable, walked straight past me towards the bus stop on the main road.

I retreated down a quiet side street to consider what to do next. Relief at having avoided a difficult encounter was starting to give way to feelings of betrayal. It was humiliating. Waldek had warned me not to get too involved but I had ignored him and here I was sneaking around, rebuffed and unable to decide on my next move.

'What are you doing, you idiot?' Having shaken off her ex at the bus stop Aśka had tailed back to find me loitering morosely in a back street. 'I am sorry but he insisted on walking me to the bus stop. What was I supposed to do?'

I mentioned this episode to Richard and Sarah the next time we met. 'He might be back on the scene when you leave,' Sarah said archly. 'When I went to Łódź Richard kept in touch with all his exes, didn't you?'

'Only two of them, Sarah.'

'Rubbish, you're a dreadful liar. The Ruffs are all hopeless letches. Anyway, so why don't you stay on for another year and keep jealous boyfriend out of the frame.'

'I really don't fancy it.'

'You know you're being incredibly wet, don't you.'

Richard tried to speak up for me. 'I don't think that's fair Sarah.'

'Yes it is. I don't think you know what you want to do.'

'All right Sarah, that'll do.'

'Don't shush me Richard, he's being absolutely spineless. If I know Polish women Aśka will already be making plans for the wedding.'

Waldek was also slightly suspicious of Aśka's motives and urged me to be on my guard.

'In Poland women try to be very powerful. They can be very manipulative. Sometimes it's necessary to stand up to them.'

Rather than run the risk of bumping into her ex again, we decided I should stay away from Koszalin for the time being. Instead of going with Aśka to her parents for Easter, I spent the day with Waldek's relatives in Chołmża, a small town a few miles from Toruń where his father managed the local dairy. An unpleasant sweet smell hit us as soon as we stepped off the train. It was a by-product of the town's decaying sugar refinery and hung thickly over the whole town.

Waldek was clearly embarrassed that I hadn't bought any flowers for his mother and insisted I present his bouquet as if I had bought them myself. To his understandable irritation he was then obliged to translate whilst she sang my praises.

When the family sat down for the Easter breakfast Waldek's

mother placed me at the head of the table next to her and kept one eye trained on my plate throughout the meal. As soon as it became empty she descended with another egg, more ham, or another slice of the dairy's rubbery cheese.

Half a dozen eggs was considered quite normal consumption and was clearly what was expected. There was no time for dipping soldiers; Waldek's father simply removed the shell and bit into the eggs as if he were eating an apple.

When Waldek's mother and sister began clearing things away I assumed that breakfast was over. Fearing I might be sick, I had just stood up to go to the bathroom when they returned with plates of sernik (cheesecake) and summoned us back to the table.

After this it was a relief to go to church. Waldek's mother prepared a basket containing some of the leftovers from breakfast, which were to be blessed, and we joined the crowds of local people going to mass. The church was full and the service had to be relayed by loudspeaker to the crowd gathered at the entrance. Some of the men outside smoked and drank bottles of beer but stood listening patiently with the rest of the congregation. After an hour and a half of alternately sitting and standing the service ended and we shuffled stiffly outside. Something about the town reminded me of a Spaghetti Western – the Catholic Church, the sleepy town square, and the desperate appearance of some of the men, like Mexican bandits who, I imagined, could turn nasty at any moment.

On Saturday I had received a telegram from Aśka to say that the coast was clear if I still wanted to come to Koszalin. This meant catching the overnight train, and so after a short walk Waldek made my apologies to his mother and put me on a train back to Toruń before the family sat down again for dinner.

I arrived at Aśka's parents the following morning in time for another helping of cheesecake and to witness their neighbours having a water fight. This, Aśka explained, was śmigus dyngus – an Easter Monday ritual in which passers-by were attacked by men and boys brandishing squeezy bottles and buckets of water.

In the afternoon some friends of Aśka's parents – the Stopas (the Polish equivalent of Foot) – arrived for coffee and cake. The conversation was dominated by Mr Stopa, a jovial and extremely voluble police officer. I tried to follow the conversation via Aśka's translation but Mr Stopa soon wore her out. In conversation classes female students tended to let the boys do most of the talking but generally regarded them with expressions of poorly concealed contempt – the same look Professor Zielińska used when any of the Polish men in the department spoke – but Mr Stopa was clearly a superior performer. He wasn't shown any of the impatience I had come to expect from Polish matriarchs when the men talked too much and even Aśka's grandmother seemed to be enjoying herself, laughing along with his jokes and joining in the conversation.

Chapter Seven

Spring / Market Economics /
Professor Pawlik / Leaving

Spring, which there had been no sign of up to now, arrived suddenly in the week after Easter. From the iron road bridge on the bus back into Toruń the city appeared to have been transformed by it; splashes of colour from the trees masked the greyness of the buildings and even the grass had lost its deathly pallor and turned green. The vegetable stall was back and the couple who ran it were noticeably more cheerful. The undignified scramble to get a place on the bus had calmed down as people started to walk and as local women – the worst offenders – shed their winter coats, leaving more space for everyone else.

Only in my flat was there no acknowledgement of the warmer weather. Not until the end of May was the heating turned off, by which time I had got used to living in my underwear and had resorted to draping wet towels over the radiators.

Confusingly the football season seemed to be just getting underway. Jacek's business/mafia friends hired a school gymnasium in Rubinkowo and invited some of the Dutch boys and myself to make up the numbers. The game itself was always a long time getting started whilst Jacek's associates stood around in the car park smoking and comparing their new cars, but once on the pitch they took it deadly seriously, cursing and swearing when things didn't go their way – lots of cries of 'Jesus Maria' and 'Kurwa', meaning whore. The Dutch boys soon organised their own games on the one pitch belonging to the university, and for Juvenalia – the Polish equivalent of Rag Week – donned orange swimming caps for a match against a local Polish team. The Dutch team also included a few ringers – a Polish goalkeeper, me, and Phil, a new English teacher from Portsmouth Polytechnic.

After the game, whilst a group of us stood outside the student bar with our drinks, we were set upon by a small group of local youths. The ringleader hit Raymond on the head and then pushed Phil backwards over a low wall before running into the forest with the rest of his gang. Jacek was the first to respond – 'Hey! Fuck!' – and suggested arming ourselves with kitchen knives from his flat and going after our assailants. To avoid any more trouble most of us went back into the bar but there was an uneasy atmosphere inside as well. It had nothing to do with the football match, which we had lost heavily. According to Ayld the Dutch boys were simply victims of their own popularity.

'These boys feel threatened by us. We have a higher standard of living in Holland and we are dating some pretty girls. How would you like it in England if the roles were reversed. I think you might start a fight, yes?'

Looking forward, as I was, to returning to England, Phil wasn't an ideal companion. One evening in May I called for him at his room in one of the student hostels and invited him to join me for a drink. When I asked him why he had come to Poland he became rather evasive.

'Put it this way, things would have become difficult if I'd stayed. Big Brother was watching me if you know what I mean. But I say good riddance. Britain's gone to the dogs anyway.'

'But isn't there anything you miss?'

'No. It was time for me to move on. I much prefer Poland.'

After a few glasses of vodka Phil decided he could trust me and revealed that he was a member of the Socialist Worker Party, and as such regarded himself as an enemy of the state vulnerable to British Secret Intelligence. Poland offered a safe haven and respite from 'the pigs'.

But by the end of the evening his attitude had softened and the Dutch boys arrived to find us toasting our homeland and chatting like old friends.

This proved to be the high point in our relationship. Whilst Phil set about learning Polish with a view to settling in Poland permanently I was starting to think about my departure. The novelty of being an English speaker in Toruń was beginning to wear off. Waldek was preoccupied with the news that Basia was expecting a baby and had virtually stopped coming round to my flat in case he met Aśka; instead I received regular visits from a professor of Economics in the flat above wanting me to correct the English in his impenetrable conference papers.

I had also detected a decline in my own novelty value following the arrival of the Dutch boys, all of whom could also speak French and German in addition to English. This impression was confirmed when Aśka and I visited Poznan where some of her friends were studying at the university. Poznan was a much larger city with a much larger university. In the English Department students opted for either British or American English and native speaker teachers of both varieties were taken for granted. Having grown used to Waldek's wonderful hospitality it was rather disconcerting to elicit no interest whatsoever.

When I had broken my journey in Poznan in September I had seen nothing of the old town, only the dismal blocks of flats and factories in the suburbs. The Town Hall in the main square was especially ornate and at midday two metal goats appeared from behind a decorative parapet to butt their horns together. Next to this beautiful Renaissance building, in the centre of the square, the communist authorities had erected what looked like two council houses to house the city's military museum and an art gallery.

I finally plucked up the courage to tell Professor Zielińska of my intention to leave at the end of the summer term and then set about trying to get Aśka an invitation and a visa to spend the summer in England. There was also a possibility that she might be selected for the exchange programme with the university in Angers and so spend the next year in France. This took some of the pressure off of me but it didn't stop one of her friends from shooting me tragic looks every time the subject of next year was mentioned.

A visa could only be applied for at the British Embassy in Warsaw and to have any chance of being processed it was necessary to join the queue several hours before the Embassy opened. We arrived in Warsaw at dawn having travelled on the overnight train in near tropical temperatures. Despite the mild early summer weather the heaters in our carriage continued to churn out hot dry air from beneath the seats and with the lurching movements of the train the compartment felt rather like being in a tumble drier. Compared to this the reception at the Embassy was decidedly chilly – 'Why do you want to travel to Britain? How will you support yourself whilst you are there? Are you planning to work whilst you are there?' etc, etc. After the brief interview we were sent away but were told to return at four o'clock to collect the visa which would be granted.

Warsaw seemed completely different under blue skies and sunshine. The hat shop had disappeared and a thriving market had grown up around the base of the Stalinist Palace of Culture, which had previously seemed so sinister. You could now buy a ticket and take a lift to the top of the building. On the streets below Polish Fiats were now outnumbered by western makes of car and there seemed to be far more traffic on the roads than on my first visit in September. A Holiday Inn had opened across the road and signs for Warsaw's first branch of MacDonald's were everywhere. Meanwhile the old fashioned station restaurant had closed and had been replaced by aluminium tables and chairs in the busy ticket hall and a couple of fast food bars.

Toruń's progress towards a market economy seemed rather more sedate. At *Śmigielski's* supermarket the baskets had been removed after a spate of shoplifting and they'd reverted to the infuriating counter system. The service in most shops was still fairly frosty but there was a much larger selection of things to buy. A few months earlier I had queued to buy onions and potatoes but now the *Nowy Rynek* was full of stalls selling a wide range of fruit and vegetables.

To cater for the new breed of *biznesmen* an expensive looking suit shop had opened on the high street. The communist era standard issue brown suit had given way to new collections in bright colours – shades of turquoise and soft pastel pinks. For Ruud and Raymond's final presentation at the bottle factory Jacek wore a dark maroon jacket over heavily pleated black trousers. As well as Jacek and myself the presentation was also attended by their two lecturers from Holland and the unsmiling management of the factory. Their lack of enthusiasm was understandable. Having spent their four month placement drinking and chasing girls, Ruud and Raymond's business plan consisted of a few well worn economic theories – OHPs of pie charts and graphs – leading to a superbly unhelpful conclusion that none of the established solutions were applicable in the current Polish economy. Their tutors, however, seemed delighted with their work and took us all out for dinner to celebrate.

On Monday following our trip to Warsaw I arrived at Collegium Maius to find the department in a state of great excitement. In the office the secretary greeted me with a knowing look and nodded in the direction of the man speaking on her telephone. He was a man of solid build and projected an air of importance from behind heavy framed spectacles and a professorial beard. When he had finished his telephone call he said something quickly to our secretary and then strode briskly over towards me.

'Aleksander Pawlik. You must be one of our native speakers. Yes, of course, Adam. I must apologise, I have only just arrived back from the States. How are you finding your time teaching here in Poland? Professor Zielińska tells me we will be losing you at the end of the year. What a pity.'

When I met Waldek shortly after he was euphoric.

'Have you met the professor? Professor Pawlik is back. You will see some changes now, Adam. The professor is very good at getting his own way with the Rector.'

The department did seem to be galvanised by his return – at least during his brief visits from Bydgoszcz – and even Marek the librarian appeared rejuvenated.

Professor Pawlik was soon followed by two grey suited professors from his university in California. Normal classes were suspended for a morning so that they could talk to the students about their respective fields – the Mappa Mundi and Chaucer.

Of more immediate concern for the students were their final exams which mainly took the form of short, and for many of them terrifying, interviews. For Aśka's *Conversation* class I prepared topics on slips of paper about which each student was expected to speak for around ten minutes. She, I suspected, had not only seen the exam topics before the exam but also shared the information with the other students. Nearly all of them appeared embarrassingly well prepared, despite officially having only fifteen minutes to prepare. Nevertheless, even with a relatively sympathetic panel of examiners – Ewa, Bartek and myself – some of the students found the exam a terrible ordeal. One girl, known to the other students as *Piggy*, had come up in an enormous rash under the pressure and another girl froze completely and was asked to come back and try again at the end of the afternoon. The students addressed themselves mainly to me; I was their teacher for conversation, and they probably thought I would be a more sympathetic ear than the Polish teachers. In attempting to achieve the appearance of proper detachment, Aśka unfortunately went so far the other way – emphatically turning her chair round to face only Ewa and Bartek – that it rather gave the game away.

Before I left at the end of June I decided to hold a party and placed a general invitation on the department notice board. Aśka helped round up a good number of students, most of whom arrived punctually and sat rather formally round the sides of the room, reluctant to accept anything to eat or drink.

Richard, who with Sarah was also one of the first to arrive, congratulated me on the arrangements.

'It's good to see things set out properly – the bread already cut and a table cloth. Well done. It feels like the parties I used to go to in York.'

'Just listen to you going on about bread and tablecloths. Please shut up,' said Sarah. 'Perhaps we should set the example and start eating some of it. Someone's got to.'

Not until the Dutch boys arrived with a sack full of beer did the party come to life. Jacek arrived with Radek and later in the evening I noticed the strange boy they referred to as *Devil* with one of Aśka's friends.

Mr Krzeszewski made a brief appearance, but otherwise from the department only Waldek and Bartek came. I hadn't seen Bartek so animated before. At one point, at the sound of their raised voices, I rushed from the kitchen expecting to see Waldek and Bartek squaring up to one another, only to find them laughing and joking. When I arrived Waldek switched into English for my benefit.

'Bartek ate your chicken. *The man's an animal, Waldek.* Do you remember? Ah Adam you must forgive us. You are leaving us in a few days time. How will you transport all your things to the station – you must let me help you.'

In the kitchen Richard had attracted a small audience of female students and was taking them to task for their passivity and lack of intellectual curiosity. Sarah had left early to collect Tashka from Basia, leaving him free to hold forth. It was a warm evening but Richard was still dressed in his tight black jeans and a long sleeved shirt and his face was flushed after drinking. He was eventually interrupted when our long-haired Polish goalkeeper picked up the guitar and started singing Bob Marley songs and the party ended, as often seemed to be the case, with someone singing *Knocking on Heaven's Door*.

Waldek held me to his promise of a lift to the station. Instead of hiring a large taxi we squeezed ourselves and all my luggage into his little Fiat. Sagging under our combined weight it stalled on the tramline which ran outside our apartment block. With a tram bearing down on us Waldek just managed to get us going in time and we shot off the grassy tramlines and lurched down the road. Black clouds which had gathered in the sultry afternoon unleashed a violent downpour just as we were beginning the short journey. By the time we reached the station Waldek was mopping the perspiration from his brow – there had been the close shave with the tram and then having to fiddle with the controls for the wipers and the heater for the windscreen…

In September the last leg of the journey from Poznań to Toruń had seemed like travelling to the end of the world. For nearly three hours we had passed nothing larger than a village and I had begun to wonder whether a university town could possibly exist so far east. As usual on the return journey the distance felt much shorter. The short storm had cleared and by the time we reached Poznań the sun had dried everything out. When the train to Ostend arrived I found that most of my compartment was occupied by an enormous Bulgarian – an architect from Sofia travelling to Berlin. Fortunately he seemed to prefer standing up and spent most of the journey blocking the corridor outside staring out of the window.

Sun streamed into the compartment as we rumbled towards the East German border. Every so often it illuminated a formation of brightly painted garden gnomes sold at the side of the road for the benefit of German motorists.

Most of the passengers left the train in Berlin just as it was getting dark. After that I had the compartment and virtually the carriage to myself.

Chapter 8

Coming Back / PGCE / The Shoe Box / Vodka

Two years later I returned to Poland perched uncomfortably on a deck chair in the aisle of a Polish tourist bus bound for Aśka's home town Koszalin. She had been engaged as an interpreter and tour guide for a cut price tour operator sending coaches of Polish tourists to countries in Western Europe. Unfortunately, all of the coaches were full so the driver found me a deck chair and I tried to make myself comfortable and not too conspicuous at the front of the bus.

If my first year in Poland had been a way of avoiding the inevitability of a PGCE (Post Graduate Certificate of Education), this second was a flight from the reality of secondary school teaching – or at least my perception of it, formed during twelve weeks of teaching practice at a school in Eastwood, an old mining town to the north of Nottingham. Its one claim to fame / point of interest was that it was D H Lawrence's birthplace.

In the half-term break, during my stint at Eastwood, I had visited Aśka in Toruń and bumped into Professor Zielińska in the Collegium Maius.

'Oh, it's you, Adam. I expect you want to come back to the

university to teach.'

Compared to the prospect of the alternative – daily humiliation at the hands of thirteen and fourteen year olds – it had seemed a reasonably attractive option and, with little hesitation, I arranged to come back for the next academic year.

'You will have to find your own accommodation, I am afraid. I am sure you can manage that yourself.'

And that was that.

It had taken just two brushes with the harsh realities of commerce to convince me that my immediate future lay on the PGCE, and beyond that in school teaching. Although I had no idea what it involved, publishing had seemed like the sort of career which might suit me. An advert for a job at Harper Collins mentioned Eastern Europe and the desirability of a background in TEFL. Any illusions I might have had that I was the ideal candidate were dispelled after a half hour interview with the HR woman at their office in Hammersmith. She clearly knew what she was doing and it probably didn't take much working out that I wasn't the person to put in charge of an 'account', even as low key as EFL text books in Poland and Czechoslovakia. Confusingly I then spent several hours with my would-be bosses, a man and a lady in their 50s, who introduced me to the entire team, and then spoke at length about the success of their department, the unique chemistry they enjoyed as managers, and their hopes for the expanding East European market. Had the meeting with the HR woman gone better that I thought? Perhaps she had given them the thumbs up and I was experiencing some sort of early induction.

Obviously not. The HR lady did know her stuff and two

days later I received a letter thanking me for my interest in the company but regretfully informing me that on this occasion I had been unsuccessful.

The other route into publishing was Media Sales. I rang a recruitment agency and was immediately invited for an interview at their office in Soho. I was shown to an upstairs room and left to wait a few minutes for the interviewer, who was on a call. The absurdity of my situation suddenly dawned on me. I had no idea what I was doing. What was Media Sales and why would I want to do it anyway? The sound of footsteps on the stairs inspired a panicky sinking sensation and I proceeded to gibber nervously and incoherently through the twenty minute interview.

The penny had dropped – this wasn't for me – and I phoned the recruitment agency the next day to withdraw my interest. By comparison, the prospect of returning to the familiar setting of an educational establishment, seemed much more attractive.

The PGCE course had begun with a three-week placement at a primary school. I was attached to a Year 5 class under the patient supervision of Mrs Hunter. Despite committing a number of teaching faux pas, which made her life more difficult, she remained remarkably friendly and supportive throughout. In my first PE lesson I immediately suggested I take the boys for football not realising – as she was quick to point out – that this wasn't the 1970s or how things worked any more. The following morning I arrived to school late, just as the Class Five bus for swimming was pulling away. The children on the back row waved at me as I sprinted after the bus, but if I thought that my dignity had suffered as a result, the day had barely started. Ten minutes into the swimming lesson a small boy, who I had been asked to escort to the toilet, spotted a trail of muddy footprints around the perimeter of the pool – made, he also spotted, by my muddy trainers. He reported this with great glee to Mrs Hunter and I was sent off to find a mop and a bucket from the attendants. I returned, barefooted, to mop the side of the pool, silently cursing my stupidity and the boy's sharp eyes.

The primary school placement was my first experience of the parsimoniousness of a school staffroom. Not only was the one teaspoon attached to the hot water urn by a chain, staff were expected to pay twenty pence for every cup of tea or instant coffee. When I returned one lunchtime with a baked potato from a café down the road, one of the older female members of staff commented on my extravagance, along the lines of 'students these days!' Needless to say her regular pack lunch consisted of several pieces of Ryvita and a small pot of yoghurt, which she scraped away at with a plastic spoon.

Having spent the first week trying to be helpful, in week two we were expected to take charge of some of the children. Perhaps as a way of testing my mettle, Mrs Hunter included a particularly troubled and troublesome boy called Steven in the withdrawal group I was to teach before lunch. This only consisted of half a dozen pupils but still ran into trouble. It began calmly enough but ended with Steven storming out and shouting 'You're a wanker' at me over his shoulder, in ear shot of the headmaster and deputy head, who had just arrived on the scene.

Fortunately, I was spared Steven when I took charge of the whole class for a morning at the end of week three. Somewhat pretentiously the theme I chose for this was the 'new Europe', and the activities included a child-friendly introduction to communism, making your own identity card / passport, and a spy game played on squared paper, along the lines of battleships.

The final six weeks of teaching practice in Eastwood were even more painful than the first six. Nothing on the PGCE course had prepared me for the consequences of resembling one of the characters from the film *Ghostbusters*. Cries of 'Egon' – my character and new name – dogged my every move at the Lower School, and when I and the other PGCE students did an assembly for years 7 and 8, it was disrupted by shouts of 'Who you gonna call?' and football-style chants of 'Eeeee-gon' from the back of the gymnasium.

This campaign of terror was led by a boy called Darren in Year 8. I only taught his class once a week – last lesson on Thursday – but it was enough to establish my reputation as the bloke from Ghostbusters. In our final lesson together one of the girls announced that they had a surprise for me – a cue for Darren and his henchmen to open fire on me with pretend slime guns in the manner of the Ghostbusters.

(A few years later, when I started teaching at a boys' comprehensive school in London, Egon returned to haunt me during a cover lesson with a Year 10 group. Unwisely I admitted that it wasn't the first time the likeness had been spotted, which had the effect of emboldening my tormentors. To a new teacher a class of Year 10 students (15 year olds) can seem like mature and intimidating adversaries, and bruised by this encounter I sought the help and sympathetic ear of the Deputy Head – a slightly humiliating interview as it involved explaining my connection to the Ghostbusters. The ringleaders were made to apologise but the nickname stuck and quickly passed down the school to the younger years, and would be given fresh impetus every time ITV showed the film – which was far too often for comfort. When, in September, I walked across the Lower School playground at the start of each new academic year I got used to listening out for the whispering of Year 7 boys, excitedly pointing that bloke from Ghostbusters to their friends.)

It didn't help that I hadn't got a clue what to teach or how to plan a lesson. I travelled to the school each day with two student history teachers, whose job appeared to consist of simply guiding the pupils through a text book – read the text in the box, now answer the questions below, etc. Unfortunately, English teaching seemed to rely almost entirely on the teacher's own devices, with the occasional freebie in the shape of watching a film version of the set texts. All of which meant many unhappy hours in my room in the hall of residence staring at a blank piece of paper, trying desperately to think of what to do. When my tutor, Colin, came to observe me teaching a Year 10 class I threw the kitchen sink into my lesson plan and achieved total confusion. From the front of the classroom I could hear Colin talking to the girls on the back row about what they had been asked to do, and then each one admitting they hadn't the slightest idea.

Towards the end of the twelve week placement I resorted to the desperate measure of faking an eye infection with the aid of my contact lens cleaning solution. Before disposable lenses were commonplace, contact lens wearers went through a nightly ritual of cleaning lenses in one solution and then leaving them to soak in another. Putting lenses in straight from the cleaning solution was agony and a mistake one was unlikely to make a second time. It left you with angry bloodshot eyes for at least the next half hour – long enough for me to call round to the house of one of the teachers in the department, and ask her to convey my apologies to the Head of Department: I wouldn't be in school for a couple of days because I had a nasty eye infection.

A better solution than self-harming would have been to copy what the qualified teachers in the department were doing – simple expedients like setting the class some work which they had some chance of being able to do. Sharon, the Head of Special Needs and a brilliant teacher, tactfully suggested we team-teach the low ability Year 8 group, to whom I had been attempting (and failing) to introduce a number of clever, but completely useless, media concepts in my weekly lesson before lunch on Friday. Her lessons involved prosaic concepts like spelling and punctuation but somehow she managed to have the class eating out of her hand.

The relief of finishing teaching practice inspired a prodigious drinking session with my fellow student teachers, and I awoke late for my last day to find I'd missed my lift and that I was incapable of speech. When I finally got to school after an expensive taxi ride up a stretch of the M1, I still wasn't capable of stringing a sentence together. My one lesson with the low ability Year 8 group loomed large. Without a lesson plan or the power of speech I was just starting to consider making a run for it when Sharon found me hiding in a corner of the Lower School staffroom. Would I mind terribly if she took the lesson today as there was something she'd promised to do with them. With some effort I managed not to cry, mumbled some words of thanks, and then sank back into my chair where I stayed for the remainder of my last day at the school.

This time there was, as Professor Zielińska had warned, no spacious flat provided for me by the university. Two years earlier, it had only been because the American teacher on the Fulbright programme had insisted on having a flat with a telephone that I had ended up living in a building occupied by senior members of the university hierarchy. The flat above mine had housed the Rector of the university, the Polish equivalent of the Vice-Chancellor.

Rather than stay in a single cell-like room in one of the student hostels, I took the professor's advice and made my own arrangements – or rather Aśka had done it for me. Viewed from the outside our flat looked like a shoe box and it was hard to believe we lived in such a small space. And instead of bumping into distinguished elderly academics on the stairs, our building was a magnet for local teenage ne'er-do-wells, who hung around outside, sometimes, it seemed, for the purpose of practicing their English swearing into our intercom. Our immediate neighbours also quickly introduced themselves, first through the thin walls with cries of 'Kurwa!' and other drunken cursing, and then in person at our door asking to borrow money, allegedly to buy some onions.

Another unwelcome change, which became obvious to me after a few days back in Toruń, was that I would also need to supplement my income. This time I had no pounds with me, and the zloty seemed to be losing value fast. In my first year I had lived quite comfortably on my university salary of just over a million zloty a month – which was about the same as £90.

Now, even when private teaching boosted my monthly income up to around six million zloty (£150 roughly), rising prices meant that I was probably worse off.

A chance meeting with my former student Jacek – long since given his marching orders by the university but now running the English programme for a bank school – seemed to provide a short-term solution to my precarious finances.

'Fuck the university! And fuck the professor! I don't give a shit about them. I am making money now. I bought this suit last week in Warsaw. If you need to borrow money I can help you.'

That didn't seem a very good idea but I did ask him if he could get me a job teaching at the new bank school.

My lessons at the bank school took place at some of the worst times you could possibly teach: 7.30 on Monday morning, 7.30 on Friday evening and 4 o'clock on Saturday afternoon. I hadn't anticipated any of this when I had accepted Professor Zielińska offer to return and, on reflection, it might have been easier to plough on as one of the Ghostbusters in an English secondary school. The Monday morning lesson was especially moribund. It's hard to persuade students to speak in their own language so early in the day, let alone one in which they are beginners, and much of the lessons passed in awkward silence. In the first Saturday lesson I tried to create a more relaxed atmosphere and began by trying to pronounce their names. One particularly severe-looking girl informed me that her name was 'dobre słowo' – which in Polish means a good word. Intrigued, I asked her what it was. She repeated that it was 'dobre słowo'. Perhaps I had been fooled by the girl's icy appearance, and lurking beneath her glacial exterior was a bit of a tease. When I repeated something to the effect of 'Come on, you can tell me', she folded her arms and fixed me with a withering look which seemed to say I've had enough of this nonsense. Her name was Dobrasłowa.

When term finally started at the university there were some new faces in the Department of English Philology. Professor Pawlik was back and very much in charge and the Polish male teachers were walking a little taller with Professor Zielińska restored to the ranks. There were two Americans – a woman called Jennifer, funded by the Fulbright programme, and a grizzled Vietnam veteran called Gary, who claimed to specialise in Native American literature. His hearing had been badly damaged during his time in the army and all of his movements and reactions seemed to have been slowed and dulled by his experience in Vietnam. On the plus side his experience as a veteran also proved to be something of a draw in the student bars, and he quickly set about trying to win the heart of a statuesque girl studying Polish literature. Unfortunately she spoke virtually no English but Gary was happy to pursue her through the words of third parties. He christened her his 'white swan', in honour of her long neck and very white skin, and later in the year presented her with an expensive and rather tasteless crystal figure of a swan.

In my first year in Toruń I had simply tried to do a passable imitation of my own university teachers. Now my pedagogy lurched to the other end of the teaching spectrum. The penny had only dropped towards the end of teaching practice that students needed to be kept occupied, and that one way to stop a class mucking about was to make them copy something off the board. I could hardly employ this strategy with undergraduates but I did make a conscious shift away from substance, towards process.

However, in my first lesson on American Literature with the third year students, I had slipped back into my old ways. At one point I stopped talking and put on an audio tape of someone else talking about the early settlers / Pilgrim Fathers. In the evening I spoke to one of the students in a bar on the main campus, a girl called Iwona. Students rating their teachers hadn't reached Britain yet, let alone Poland, but she didn't hold back or mince her words. 'Totally boring' was her assessment.

From then on my lessons largely consisted of party games – adapted to suit various literary texts – and I deemed them a success if the students appeared reasonably happy and involved. This wasn't always possible given the depressed state of some of my students, but from that point on lessons were generally less funereal.

One night late in October I was woken in the middle of the night by our doorbell. The fact that it was buzzing continuously added to the sense of confusion and panic. I opened the front door to find our neighbour leaning against the doorbell, asleep, reeking of vodka and drunk. Had it not been for the noise of the doorbell I might have been tempted to leave him there propped up against the wall. Instead I turned him so that he was facing his door and gave him a gentle shove in that direction. Fortunately he was quietly cooperative and shuffled unsteadily towards his door without protest or the usual cries of 'kurwa!'

The other hazard attached to living in our flat were the many unattended local dogs, which patrolled the area between our front door and a parade of shops fifty yards away. A group of Dachshunds, who collected around the steps to the shops, were an especially hostile presence and barked furiously at anyone going in and out of the shops.

I had my own brush with vodka on the 1 November national holiday. Gary had introduced me to a young law teacher from England, and when Aśka returned to her parents for the annual family gathering at the cemetery, I sought him out. Simon was clearly enjoying himself and was not inconvenienced by the need to do much teaching. Unfortunately I still had a conversation class the following morning with a group of very pleasant second year students. This became rather forgotten as the night wore on, but by the time I stumbled out of the student bar at the end of the evening it wasn't the only thing to have been blanked out. Heavy snow fall had obliterated the landmarks by which I might have hoped to find my way home and condemned me to several hours of unproductive sliding and slithering through deserted streets which now all looked the same. Conditions were treacherous underfoot, especially for someone in my befuddled state, and I repeatedly found myself sprawled face down in the snow. The thirty minute walk home took the best part of three hours and I arrived home to the shoe box exhausted and soaking wet.

I woke to find that I had lost the power of speech (again) but foolishly set off for the Collegium Maius for my conversation class. By the time I managed to stagger up to the third floor the students were already gathered in the corridor. Fortunately explanations were unnecessary; they took one look at me and then escorted me to the coffee shop in the basement, where, after about half an hour, I was able to join their conversation.

The mistake I had made had been not eating enough. Later in the year I attended the wedding of one of Aśka's friends and on the tables at the reception there seemed to be a bottle of vodka for every two people. Mindful of my disaster on the November holiday I was reluctant to partake. However, it soon became obvious that the vodka was necessary to wash down the endless procession of food. When the first plate of hot food arrived I tucked in eagerly and polished it off, not realising that more would be arriving at fifteen minute intervals for the next four hours. I also managed most of the bottle of vodka on my own but this time woke with a strange sense of having been purified, but also felt very tired.

The job of injecting a bit of fun / any sort of life into the bank school lessons was much harder than with the university students. The snow, which had fallen on the 1st November, remained to various degrees until the end of March and made getting up for the bus to the Monday morning lesson even harder. Their English wasn't up to conversation so I fell back on resources I'd previously used with Spanish school children on EFL summer schools, particularly the *Pair Work* books. Unfortunately, this involved lots of photocopying. This no longer entailed visits to the basement of Collegium Maius to see the surly keeper of the photocopier, but remained an obstacle to my pedagogy. Sometimes, in my desperation to get through the hour and a half lessons, I paid to have my copying done in a shop in town, just so that Dobroslawa and her bank school colleagues could place various kitchen equipment on their empty drawing of a kitchen, or mark the symbols for weather on their maps of the UK. These functional tasks at least generated a low hum of conversation, whilst I looked on relieved not to be trying to explain the grammar points in their course book.

At some point before Christmas it began to occur to me – as it hadn't ever done during the year in Nottingham on the PGCE – that teaching wasn't quite so bad after all, and that it could actually be quite enjoyable. Instrumental in this shift in thinking was Giles, a wandering English Language teacher who was employed by the British Council to teach at the teacher training college – a real teacher earning a real salary, which couldn't be said of most of the 'native speakers' teaching in Toruń. He was camp and acerbic in equal measure, and, long before anyone had heard of Strictly Come Dancing was being Craig Revel-Hall to his enchanted students and colleagues.

Giles was also a brilliant linguist and, despite only having just arrived in Poland, quickly overtook me in his grasp of the Polish language. Having acquired a thorough knowledge of the vocabulary needed to buy vegetables at the market, my Polish had stalled. I hadn't even managed to master the pronunciation for the word three ('trzy') and often resorted to asking for two of something and then asking for one more just to avoid it.

Together with a young American Peace Corps teacher called John, and Eric, one of the Dutch business students from my first year in Toruń who had stayed, we engaged Andrzej to teach us Polish. Like most of the university students studying English, Andrzej was able to make money from teaching English to Polish school children, but was out of his depth trying to teach confident linguists like Giles and Eric. Fairly soon we also found ourselves working from exercises copied from Pair Work – giving Giles instructions in my dodgy Polish on how 'to get to the Post Office from the Bank', and where he should place the sofa in his empty living room etc. After three increasingly desperate lessons we invited Andrzej to Pod Aniołem, a new bar in the basement beneath the old Town Hall, and tried to explain to him, as gently as possible, that we felt that we'd come as far as we could under his teaching.

The impenetrability of the Polish language continued to torment me on a daily basis. The ladies in our local shop were especially unsympathetic to useless foreigners. On one occasion I asked them if they had any mayonnaise, which prompted lots of head shaking, tutting and baffled looks of disapproval. Sure as I was that the word for mayonnaise was the same in Polish, I doggedly repeated the enquiry several times, but got the same response. Eventually I spotted a jar of mayonnaise on a shelf behind the counter and pointed to it eagerly, feeling vindicated.

'Ah! May-*on*-ez.'

I hadn't quite stressed the middle syllable enough for their liking.

The Polish for corn flakes (płatki kukurydziane) involved a seven syllable tongue twister which I was unable to master so I had to rely on pointing.

Chapter 9

Hospital / Winter School / Zakopane / Leaving

One day towards the end of January, just before the February university holiday, the department's secretary found me at my desk in a state of some distress. The day had begun normally enough, but by the time I had got off at the tram stop near Collegium Maius I had the beginnings of a headache. An hour later, when I was found by Danuta, I was huddled over my desk in my coat shaking uncontrollably. Danuta went to fetch Waldek, who whisked me away in his small Fiat to the hospital.

A female doctor with dyed orange hair poked and prodded my chest whilst Waldek looked on anxiously. The diagnosis – 'It might be pneumonia' – wasn't really the reassurance I was looking for. I was given an array of enormous looking tablets and told to stay in bed for five days. When Aśka was doing her private teaching, this unfortunately meant quite a bit of time in the sofa bed next to the dividing wall with the drunk neighbours, attempting to get rest and recuperation through the screams and bumps and cries of 'Kurwa!'

A more serious problem was that I was due to travel to Vienna in three days' time to teach on a Winter School course run by my local EFL college in England – a chance to earn some hard currency I couldn't afford to pass up. Trusting that the suspected pneumonia was simply further proof of Polish pessimism in matters of health, I decided to attempt the journey. I arrived in Warsaw in one piece, and visited the new Pizza Hut next to the Marriot Hotel building, but struggled to finish a child-size pizza.

At the airport we were bused across the tarmac in driving rain to a tiny and ancient-looking Lufthansa plane with propellers. It scarcely looked capable of getting the contents of the bus and its team of very tall German stewardesses into the air, but once on board everything proceeded with metronomic efficiency. Lunch was served immediately. Amongst the many cellophane-wrapped condiments and items of cutlery, there was also a miniscule metal bull clip. When the unsmiling stewardess arrived with the coffee I asked her what it was for, but my attempt at light-heartedness was instantly rebuffed.

'It is for your napkin. To clip it to your tie,' she replied briskly, and then moved on imperiously with the silver coffee jug.

I was collected in Vienna by the course leader, and after a quick change of clothes in the quaint guest house which was to be our base, taken to a ball given by the headmaster as a welcome to the visiting English teachers. To wash down what would be the first of many Wiener schnitzels over the next fortnight, I drank a lot of the local red wine and then, at the jovial headmaster's insistence, some Schnapps. I woke the next morning feeling in perfect health, and after a hearty breakfast went for long walk.

The only choice at breakfast was between white or brown roles, strawberry jam or marmalade, and between tea and coffee. Nevertheless the process of ordering breakfast (there were only four of us staying there) usually took ten minutes as our landlady enquired minutely as to our night's sleep, and explored variations on the theme of My Fair Lady, her favourite English language film. For some reason she had addressed me as the 'Colonel' on my arrival and then subsequently, and so my roommate, John, became Professor Higgins and was asked to judge her English pronunciation – 'The rain in Spain' etc.

Peter, a retired prep school master, who had taught on the Winter School before, spoke ambitiously about putting on an end of course show. I was relieved to find that he wasn't banking on contributions from everyone else; I appeared to have been given the beginners group – fifteen thirteen year old boys whose only interests appeared to be football and what they were having for lunch – invariably Wiener schnitzel and chips. Time hung heavy and in order to get through the long mornings I was obliged to top-up the course book with all of my favourite TEFL time fillers – Pair Work, the Yes/No game, Give Us A Clue, Fizz Bong (a converted drinking game), Blockbusters and Ship or Sheep – a form of pedagogical torture for language students requiring them to differentiate between long (sheep) and short (ship) vowel sounds.

After lunch it was permissible, after a respectable interval for work, to take them out to the playground for a game of football. This got earlier and earlier as the two weeks progressed and as my interest, and their interest in learning English, waned. A central tenet of secondary school life in Austria – or at least in this school – was that no one was allowed to wear shoes. Outdoor shoes were exchanged for felt slippers by staff and students alike on arrival at the school, which allowed me to waste even more time every time we went out to the playground.

When I got back to Toruń with my modest stash of pounds I set about trying to shed my bank school commitments. Giles, meanwhile, was considering taking on extra teaching, in order to pay off a mysteriously large phone bill. Although obviously gay, Giles was guarded about his private life. I surprised him one evening by calling unannounced at his flat. He had company – a young Polish man with big brown eyes and Tunisian appearance, who didn't appear to speak any English, and who I later surmised was the cause of the enormous phone bill. Giles betrayed no embarrassment at this slightly awkward meeting and introduced me to his friend, but never referred to him subsequently. It clearly wasn't the moment to hang around and I left as quickly as possible. The phone bill, however, continued to be a topic of conversation and consternation for some time, understandably given that it was in excess of £1000 – more than my university salary for the year and some achievement in old zloty.

By Easter I had managed to extricate myself entirely from the Bank School. The last of the snow had finally melted away and a spell of warm weather coincided with the start of the holiday – in Toruń, at least.

Alistair and his girlfriend Fiona, along with two other friends from England, William and Astrid, had booked a New Millennium coach holiday in Zakopane – a mountain resort south of Krakow. Aśka and I travelled to Zakopane to meet them, naively expecting the same spring weather, and, in my case, packing nothing warmer than a short denim jacket.

The train from Krakow wound slowly south in depressing drizzle but within an hour of our arrival we were trudging through a snow blizzard. Snow continued to fall heavily through the night and by the time the New Millennium bus arrived around midnight – hours later than it should have done after a long delay in Germany – winter had been fully restored.

On our previous visit to Zakopane, two summer ago, Aśka and I had bought matching coarse woollen jumpers and socks from the market selling traditional mountain wares. We didn't regret this rash purchase quite as quickly as Alistair had his Solidarity umbrella, but it was enough to try on a single sock – a feeling akin to wrapping yourself up in wire wool – to realise there was no way we would ever wear any of it. Now, though, we might have overlooked the discomfort if it had meant having another layer to keep out the cold. I was obliged to borrow extra jumpers to pad out my flimsy denim jacket and had to resort to wearing plastic bags inside my shoes to keep my feet dry.

None of my friends were remotely well-off, but such was the strength of the pound against the zloty that Aśka and I felt like the poor relations. One evening, to try to redress the balance, I bought a bottle of vodka and made Bloody Marys for everyone, intended as a little treat before we went out in the evening. The absence of ice immediately rendered it unacceptable to Alistair, and the others quickly formed a similar opinion. To be fair, without ice the tomato juice looked and tasted like cold tomato soup, and nor had I provided any of the other ingredients – lemon, pepper, tabasco etc. – which make it enjoyable, and it all ended up being thrown away.

Their itinerary included a night in Krakow at the end of

the week, and we met up with them again in the old town square for a meal before returning to Toruń. They insisted on paying for everything – ostensibly as a thank you to Aśka for translating menus and generally showing them the ropes – but also because they could quite easily afford it.

Being a zloty millionaire, I realised, wasn't getting me very far. The time had come to go back to England and get a proper job, and at the start of June I started applying for teaching jobs in schools in the north London area.

Before I left Toruń, Professor Pawlik invited Gary and I for lunch. In between mouthfuls of pork knuckle he managed to put us both on the spot by asking, 'So, which of our girls are you taking away with you?' I had to admit that Aśka would be following me to England in a few weeks when she'd completed her degree. Gary's planning was less advanced – 'Yes sir. I hope so sir.' – but he was still pinning his hopes on his white swan.

Chapter 10

Two Interviews / A Job

One advantage, I told myself, of applying for teaching jobs so late in the school year was that schools would be becoming anxious to fill vacant positions and might be less choosy. Notwithstanding this logic I only heard back from two schools.

My first interview was at a high achieving mixed school near Watford. Everything about the school seemed deadly serious, especially the chilly Head of Department, who refused to smile or acknowledge me or the other candidate as we sat nervously in the reception area, despite walking past us half a dozen times. He did finally speak to me in the interview and, sounding rather sceptical, asked me to expand on a claim I'd made in my letter of application – something about having developed ingenious and inclusive methodologies during my time teaching in Poland. Given that this really boiled down to playing various party games, I found myself blustering in an attempt to present my personalised methodology in a more progressive light. He looked distinctly unimpressed and left the rest of the interview to the Head and Deputy Head.

We weren't allowed to eat our school dinner in the canteen,

but were shown to what looked like a police interview room, where we were to eat and then wait whilst they deliberated. Eventually it was left to the Head to inform us that neither of us were really what the school was looking for. We passed the Head of Department on our way out. He walked straight past us and said nothing.

Watford, I consoled myself, wasn't an ideal location for someone staying with friends in Crouch End, but it wasn't a great start.

Fortunately my second interview was at a boys' grammar school – although it actually turned out to be a comprehensive school – which was rather less fussy. The Head of Department took me for a walk around the school grounds and then to the pub, which appeared to be almost an extension of the school buildings, and which I later discovered was referred to as the 'Annexe'. I sipped a coke whilst he polished off three pints of Stella Artois, and was then taken to see the elderly Headmaster in his musty study. On the desk in front of him was my CV, but every time he put his glasses on and looked down at it, apparently about to ask me a question, he removed them again and carried on reminiscing about football and cricket. This continued very pleasantly for about an hour, at the end of which he had only asked me a single question, but concluded that 'Everything seems perfectly satisfactory' and promised to contact me the next day with a firm offer.

Rather less satisfactory, I discovered later, was that the school was being inspected during the first week of term. Unlike the short notice (twenty-four hours), small scale Ofsted visits today, the school had had several months to prepare, although there were no obvious signs of any advanced planning. The

Head of RE (referred to by other members of staff as Sir Les) had returned to find his classroom stripped bare, in the middle of being re-painted, and spent the two Inset Days before Ofsted arrived bemoaning his plight to anyone who would listen.

My Head of Department had prepared a departmental pamphlet designed principally it seemed to disguise any shortcomings behind a cloak of isms and high-brow intellect. He also told me not to worry about the inspectors; I was an NQT (newly qualified teacher) and they wouldn't be interested in what I was doing, and probably wouldn't even observe me. In fact the English inspector visited four of my lessons. The first occasion was in Sir Les' freshly painted room – last lesson of the day with a difficult Year 8 class. As well as the English inspector there was another inspector watching the Teaching Assistant supporting me. As soon as the class and various adults had settled down in their seats, the Turkish boy, who the TA was there to support / restrain, put his hand up.

'Yes, what is it, Mehmet?' I asked patiently.

'Sir, are you frigid?'

Not knowing how to respond to this in this company I pretended I hadn't heard and launched into my Learning Objectives for the lesson.

By Thursday afternoon the inspection was supposed to have been done and dusted, and I judged it safe to put on the film of *Of Mice and Men* for the little bottom Year 11 group I was teaching in period five. Not only did I not have any Learning Objectives, or a lesson plan of any sort, because of the wooden floors and high ceilings in my classroom it was also virtually impossible to hear what George and Lennie were saying. Ten minutes into the film the inspector walked in and sat down at the back of the room.

Trying not appear too rattled I let the film play for another couple of minutes and then, very deliberately stopped it and asked the boys, who had been huddled round the TV, to return to their desks and open their exercise books. Recalling something I'd done with the American Literature students in Toruń on the Garden of Eden / creation symbolism at the start of the novel, I asked the class to draw a lizard, followed by a rabbit.

Had the inspector not left at this point, the rabbit would have been followed by a racoon, a dog, a deer, and then a man – re-creating, I was prepared to argue rather pointlessly, the creation story in the Book of Genesis. As it was I decided it was safe to put the film back on, and let it play for the rest of the lesson.

Despite my contribution to the inspection, I had joined – it was announced on Friday morning – a 'Good' school.

Postscript

January 2018 – Another Gap / Gardening Leave

Fittingly it is a filthy Monday morning. Pathetic fallacy springs to mind as I drive through pouring rain to drop my children off for school. Not wanting to tell them what has happened I dressed in my work clothes and gave the impression that I was going to school as usual. This reminds me of a news report I saw years ago about Japanese businessmen and bankers who lost their jobs in the financial slump of the 1980s. Rather than face telling their families the bad news they continued going off in the mornings in their suits and with their attaché cases, but actually spent the days in a public park chatting with other men in the same boat.

My choice of poem for the Christmas mock exam – *Kamikaze* – now seems rather appropriate, or, in English teacher terms, a clear case of foreshadowing or dramatic irony.

Later I walked to the post office and bought a paper. I am not the only one in a spot of bother it seems. Ant, as in Ant and Dec, is facing a £31 million divorce bill, and my son texts me with the latest about the England cricketer Ben Stokes – 'Stokes charged with add ray' – which turns out to be 'affray'. It is also apparently Blue Monday – officially trumpeted at the most miserable day of the year – which again feels apt.

Among the small ads in the window of the post office is one for a 'Traditional Window Cleaner', whatever that is. Presumably it means a man with a bucket and a ladder, as opposed to a high pressure hose.

Thursday 18 January = E plus one. 'E' for end, possibly, of my days as a teacher.

The E should stand for exams, and was the catchphrase of one of my old colleagues, drummed into GCSE students in the countdown towards their final exams – E-74, E-73, and so on. One cohort responded on their first day of freedom / study leave by daubing 'E+1' in enormous letters on the wall of the Sports Hall, and, for good measure, locking the main school gates with an industrial strength padlock so that the fire brigade had to be called to open the school.

After my meeting yesterday I think it is unlikely I'll be going back. I have landed myself in hot water – or the 'soup' as Captain Grimes calls it in *Decline and Fall*. Unlike Captain Grimes, I don't have a letter from my housemaster ensuring me against disaster and of my safe passage into my next teaching post.

Yesterday evening my son tried to put a positive spin on my ubiquitous presence around the house, describing me as the 'midwife', although I think he meant house wife. He has already started taking advantage of the situation and secured a lift nearly to the gates of his own school this morning. Similarly my wife, whose parting words this morning concerned the toilet seat in the downstairs loo which she wants changing.

Later I had a short and unsuccessful engagement with the

old toilet seat, which refused to budge, despite my efforts on all fours with the pliers and adjustable spanner. But it should be possible to smarten up the old one and I will go in search of metal polish and linseed oil this afternoon with a renewed sense of purpose – my *aims and objectives*.

Meanwhile I seem to have found a new *starter* activity to begin the day, courtesy of my cat – sweeping up mouse remains which he has deposited, very considerately, on the front door step.

After that I set about trying to forestall my wife's manic round of Saturday cleaning by doing the hoovering and cleaning the toilets. It isn't actually quite as straightforward as that and in relation to the hoovering she is especially vigilant. If I am to stop her going back over what I have done it will have to pass muster.

As befits gardening leave I also pick up some sticks in the garden, brought down by last night's heavy wind. An elderly gardener is doing the same thing in next door's garden. My neighbour, who runs a building firm, is a passionate advocate for the importance of work and won't be impressed by my new enforced leisure.

In the afternoon I go into town and join the many older and retired people who are having a coffee. I overhear one couple telling a friend that they have been for a walk along the canal and deserve a coffee. Perhaps old age begins when you stop needing a coffee and start talking about deserving one.

Philip Larkin's toad poems about work – *Toads* and *Toads Revisited* – come to mind. More particularly *Toads Revisited* since I have become *'one of the men… dodging the toad work'*. I've joined the *'hare-eyed clerks'* and *'wax-fleshed out-patients'*.

I haven't quite resorted to brooding over my *'failures by some bed of lobelias'* but I have started regular afternoon walks. Freed from the tyranny of the bell and a five period day I realise I've started replacing it with new routines and have repeated the same route three days running.

Another literary reference that crops up every time my wife mentions another website advertising teaching jobs is Hibbert's cry for help in *Journey's End* – *'I swear I'll never go into those trenches again. Shoot! – and thank God'*.

THOSE WHO CAN'T...

28628050R00070

Printed in Great Britain
by Amazon